That's Why We Call Him MESSIAH

That's Why We Call Him MESSIAH

HAL SEED

CHURCHLEADERS
PRESS

Colorado Springs

That's Why We Call Him
MESSIAH

First Edition: Year 2023

Why We Call Him Messiah / Outreach, Inc.
Paperback ISBN: 978-1-958585-49-8
eBook ISBN: 978-1-958585-51-1

CHURCHLEADERS
PRESS

Colorado Springs

CONTENTS

INTRODUCTION

All of us have had them.

Moments when everything changed.

You didn't see it coming, but something happened.

- You read something that changed how you see things.
- An elder's words changed how you see yourself.
- An outstanding grade or performance caused you to realize you were smart, or fast, or strong.

History records 101 people who had personal encounters Jesus. Most of them had moments like these. (For my listing of **101 Personal Encounters with Jesus**, see the End Notes.)

For hundreds of years, Jewish prophets foretold the coming of "The Anointed One," the *Messiah*. Why is it that the majority of those who ate with, talked with, watched, or just listened to Jesus, were so touched by the encounter that they concluded he was the Messiah?

That's what we'll explore in the pages that follow. We'll look at the lives of six people: a skeptical follower, an ashamed woman, a desperate father, a loving sister, a rabbinical scholar, and a career soldier. Each of them came away convinced Jesus was not only the Messiah, but the Son of God and Savior of the world.

It seems unlikely, maybe even impossible. Yet it happened in history. All of them were altered by meeting Jesus. He has that effect on people.

In each of the fast-paced six chapters to follow, I'll also relay the story of a contemporary or historical person who was similarly changed and highlight six forms of proof—one in each chapter—that point to the conclusion that Jesus was and is the Messiah.

It's my prayer that you'll encounter Jesus as you read their stories. If you do, I can almost guarantee you'll be changed as well.

—Dr. Hal Seed

CHAPTER 1

A Disciple Who Couldn't Believe

THE STORY OF THOMAS

Nobody knows his real name. To the Greeks he was *Didymus.* Aramaic speakers called him *Thomas.* Both words mean "twin." Thomas was raised alongside a womb mate. Whether his double was male or female, nobody knows.

What we do know is that Thomas was a questioner. If he'd been raised in America, we would have said, "He's from Missouri," the *Show-Me* state. People like Thomas need to see things to believe. None of this "trust me" reasoning. They want verifiable data. Assuming is dangerous. Confirmation is king.

It's unclear precisely how Show-Me-like this young man was. Whether fair or unfair, his single iconic declaration expressing skepticism about the resurrection of Christ clung to him so tightly that history has dubbed him *Doubting Thomas.*

In an ironic turnaround, once Thomas had his doubts removed, Mr Twin became such a dedicated man of faith that large numbers of people across dozens of cultures named their sons after him. According to the U.S. Social Security, over the most recent hundred years in

America, 1.6229 million families chose "Thomas" as the designation they wanted their child known by. Add to that all the Tom, Tommy, Thompson, Thom, Tommao, Tome, Tomas, Tomaz, and Thomasinas around the world, and you can conclude that a lot of people have admired this man.

Few facts are available about the Twin's childhood. There's evidence he grew up in northern Israel, in the region known as Galilee. Galilee's most striking feature is its lake that goes by that name. Though it's only eight miles wide and thirteen miles long, this somewhat small lake is called the *Sea* of Galilee. A burst of bravado must have come upon whoever named it.

Anyway, the boy and his double grew up fishing and swimming together. When chores were done, maybe they went rafting, or lazed in the sand.

There's also evidence that the twins' father was a builder, which likely means Tom's early employment was around boards and bricks before he met Jesus. Incidentally, the New Testament word for builder is *tekton*, which is the same descriptor used for the father of Jesus. So both master and disciple grew up in the homes of construction workers. No doubt both were good at laying bricks and building houses, as well as household furniture. It's possible Thomas' dad and Jesus' dad may have worked together from time to time.

As for schooling, first-century Jewish boys entered *Bet Sepher*, akin to our elementary school, around age six. There they learned to read, using the first five books of the Bible, called *Torah*. Around age twelve most were done with formal education, dropping out and learning their father's trade.

More gifted students stayed on for another three years of *Bet Midrash*, something like our high school or college. In Bet Midrash, they learned the rest of the Jewish Bible, called *Tanakh*. To graduate from Bet Midrash, you had to memorize the entire Tanakh, so lots of students were weeded out along the way. A few made it through the whole thing. Depending on one's intelligence and tenacity, graduation from Bet Midrash could come for the gifted students somewhere between the age of fourteen and fifteen. But again, few lasted that long. If Thomas applied himself, he may have made it this far in school.

According to Dr. Ray Vander Laan, the goal of just about every boy in that culture was to continue studying and eventually become a Rabbi.[1] Reaching that level required a third level of school, called *Bet Talmud*. Only the best of the best got this opportunity. Think Harvard or Stanford. Rabbis were rare in those days. And, if and when you became one, you were very particular about who you selected to train up and to succeed you.

When he met Jesus, Thomas was not in school, which means he hadn't made it to the elite level academically. He was working in the building trade, following his father.

Then, it happened.

The gospel of Mark records that, *Jesus went up the mountain and summoned those he wanted, and they came to him. He appointed twelve, whom he called apostles, to be with him, to send them out to preach, and to have authority to drive out demons. He appointed the Twelve: To*

1 Vander Laan, Ray: *The Dust of the Rabbi* (sermon).

Simon, he gave the name Peter; and to James the son of Zebedee, and to his brother John, he gave the name "Boanerges," (that his, "Sons of Thunder"); Andrew; Philip and Bartholomew; Matthew and Thomas; James the son of Alphaeus, and Thaddeus; Simon the Zealot, and Judas Iscariot, who also betrayed him.[2]

Jesus chose Thomas to be one of his *Talmid* (student, or disciple). He was in his mid- to late-teens. For the next two-and-a-half years, young Thomas-the-Talmid followed Jesus everywhere. As we'll see in coming stories, Jesus was mesmeric. Nearly everyone was spellbound by him. But not our Twin. His *show-me* mindset restrained his exuberance. Thomas followed Jesus, *but not blindly.*

One of the most refreshing things about the Bible is, it presents its heroes sans make-up. It reveals them to us warts and all.

One of the most refreshing things about the Bible is, it presents its heroes sans make-up. It reveals them to us warts and all. Our subject, who eventually will be called *Saint* Thomas, is not a super-spiritual person. He's human. We can relate to him.

This unvarnished apostle is devoted, but pessimistic. He's genuine in his ignorance and obstinate in his unwillingness to believe without personal tangible proof, which makes his transformation from skeptic to saint all the more convincing. When he finally sees the post-resurrection Jesus for himself, his stubbornness makes him a lifelong follower despite some very trying circumstances.

2 Mark 3:13–19.

THOMAS AND JESUS

Thomas features large in three stories in the Gospels. Together, they give us a portrait of a credible and fallible young man. The Twin has his highs and his lows, climaxing in the moment when he's overcome by the evidence for Jesus' divinity.

"Let's go die with him."

The first time Thomas takes centerstage in Scripture comes in John 11. It's late winter, six or eight weeks before Christ's death. Jesus is ministering in the Jordan Valley, about twenty-five miles from Jerusalem.

Christ has come here intentionally. A few weeks earlier, at the Feast of Hanukkah, Jewish leaders had picked up stones to stone him. Jesus knew that the Lamb of God must die on the day of Passover, still several weeks away. So he withdrew to a safe distance from the dangers of Jerusalem to continue training his disciples for as long as he could.

The Lord was friends with three siblings named Mary, Martha, and Lazarus, who lived in the village of Bethany. Bethany is two miles from Jerusalem in what is called "the hill country of Judea."

The Bible doesn't say how, but one day Lazarus contracted or contacted something fatal. This was long before vaccines and antibiotics. The bug he caught or the injury he suffered took his life in a matter of days.

Distraught, the sisters sent for Jesus. "Come quickly! The one you love is sick!" When Jesus heard this, he waited two days before responding. (His reasoning was nuanced. We'll uncover it when we come back to this story in Chapter 4.)

After forty-eight hours had passed, Jesus said to his disciples, *"Let's go to Judea again."*[3] This was a dangerous idea. Those seeking his life lived not far away.

"Rabbi," the disciples told him, "just now the Jews tried to stone you, and you're going there again?"[4] The last thing they wanted was for Jesus to die.

Heated discussion ensued. After some minutes, Jesus gave the final word on the matter. *Jesus then told them plainly, "Lazarus has died. I'm glad for you that I wasn't there so that you may believe. But let's go to him."*[5]

The fellas whispered between them, "Is this wise? It doesn't seem safe." At this moment, our pessimist speaks up: *Thomas (called "Twin") said to his fellow disciples, "Let's go too so that we may die with him."*[6]

Had Thomas read *Winnie the Pooh,* Eeyore would have been his favorite character. He doesn't expect that Jesus will make it out of there alive. But, hey, if Jesus is going, then Thomas will throw his lot in with him. This is the kind of guy you'd like to have standing next to you in a brawl.

"We don't know where you're going."

Thomas' second story is less flattering. It's dinnertime. The disciples are reclining around a table in a place we've come to know as "The Upper Room." Thomas has just polished off his last morsel when Jesus

3 John 11:7.
4 John 11:8.
5 John 11:14–15.
6 John 11:16.

drops a bombshell. He's been hinting at it for weeks now, but the disciples haven't really believed him.

"Don't let your heart be troubled. Believe in God; believe also in me. In my Father's house are many rooms. If it were not so, would I have told you that I am going to prepare a place for you? If I go away and prepare a place for you, I will come again and take you to myself, so that where I am you may be also. You know the way to where I am going."[7]

You could have heard a pin drop. "Is it possible that Jesus is talking about his death? Did he really just say that? What does this mean for us?"

Again, whispers start. They escalate to full voices. For a second time, the Twin speaks up. *"Lord," Thomas said, "we don't know where you're going. How can we know the way?"*[8]

In retrospect, it seems obvious that Jesus was talking about going to heaven. But these twelve young men have invested their lives and futures with him. It's impossible to fathom that someone who can calm storms, walk on water, and feed thousands with a few loaves and fish could suffer an early death, much less any death at all.

The man with the *show-me* outlook calls for clarification. "Spell it out for us please. Where exactly are you going, sir? We would all very much like to continue following you."

Jesus explains, *"I am the way, the truth, and the life. No one comes to the Father except through me. If you know me, you will also know my Father. From now on you do know him and have seen him."*[9]

7 John 14:1–4.
8 John 14:5.
9 John 14:6–7.

I wonder what Thomas thought when he heard this. We can't get into his head, but did he finally understand the inevitability of Jesus' death? History doesn't tell us. But the third story of Thomas makes clear that he didn't expect a resurrection.

"My Lord and my God!"

It's safe to say that none of Jesus' disciples fully grasped that their leader's need to die on behalf of the world, much less, *would* actually die that very next day. Two days after his death, all four gospel accounts picture them in shock and dismay, fearing for their own lives.[10]

Luke's account provides the most detailed: *On the first day of the week, very early in the morning, they came to the tomb, bringing the spices they had prepared. They found the stone rolled away from the tomb. They went in but did not find the body of the Lord Jesus. While they were perplexed about this, suddenly two men stood by them in dazzling clothes. So the women were terrified and bowed down to the ground.*

"Why are you looking for the living among the dead?" asked the men. "He is not here, but he has risen! Remember how he spoke to you when he was still in Galilee, saying, 'It is necessary that the Son of Man be betrayed into the hands of sinful men, be crucified, and rise on the third day'?" And they remembered his words.

Returning from the tomb, they reported all these things to the Eleven and to all the rest. Mary Magdalene, Joanna, Mary, the mother of James, and the other women with them were telling the apostles these things. But these words seemed like nonsense to them, and they did not believe the

10 Luke 24:9–12, 36–49; John 20:19–25; Matthew 28:5–10; Mark 16:14.

women. Peter, however, got up and ran to the tomb. When he stooped to look in, he saw only the linen cloths. So he went away, amazed at what had happened.[11]

That's the account of Sunday morning.

Luke also describes Jesus' first in-person reunion with the disciples, which happened that same evening.

As they were saying these things, he himself stood in their midst. He said to them, "Peace to you!" But they were startled and terrified and thought they were seeing a ghost. "Why are you troubled?" he asked them. "And why do doubts arise in your hearts? Look at my hands and my feet, that it is I myself! Touch me and see, because a ghost does not have flesh and bones as you can see I have." Having said this, he showed them his hands and feet. But while they still were amazed and in disbelief because of their joy, he asked them, "Do you have anything here to eat?" So they gave him a piece of a broiled fish, and he took it and ate in their presence.

He told them, "These are my words that I spoke to you while I was still with you—that everything written about me in the Law of Moses, the Prophets, and the Psalms must be fulfilled." Then he opened their minds to understand the Scriptures. He also said to them, "This is what is written: The Messiah will suffer and rise from the dead the third day, and repentance for forgiveness of sins will be proclaimed in his name to all the nations, beginning at Jerusalem. You are witnesses of these things. And look, I am sending you what my Father promised. As for you, stay in the city until you are empowered from on high."[12]

11 Luke 24:1–12.
12 Luke 24:36–49.

John's account gives us one more important piece of information. *But Thomas (called "Twin"), one of the Twelve, was not with them when Jesus came.*[13]

When the other disciples tried to explain to poor Tom that they had actually seen Jesus in the flesh, his *show-me* nature kicked in once again. *He said to them, "If I don't see the mark of the nails in his hands, put my finger into the mark of the nails, and put my hand into his side, I will never believe."*[14]

"I need proof. I need to *see.* I need to *touch.* I cannot believe otherwise." This is the quote for which all history has labeled him *Doubting Thomas.*

Which really isn't fair. What he was being asked to believe was so contrary to logic and the laws of physics that probably most of us would have said the same thing. "That's too much to take in on trust. Crucifixion is the most thorough form of torture and death ever invented. When the Romans kill you, you are D-E-A-D, dead."

Thomas just could not take others' word that Jesus was alive. Something like that would have to be a miracle. A really *big* miracle. Miracles don't happen very often. And miracles like that had *never* happened!

So, he doubted. (So would I.)

Yet, today, this former skeptic is revered the world over as one who willingly gave his life telling people that Jesus Christ is the Savior of the world, who has risen from the dead. What happened to change his mind?

13 John 20:24.
14 John 20:25.

Here comes the moment: *A week later his disciples were indoors again, and Thomas was with them. Even though the doors were locked, Jesus came and stood among them and said, "Peace be with you."*

Then he said to Thomas, "Put your finger here and look at my hands. Reach out your hand and put it into my side. Don't be faithless, but believe."[15]

Freeze that frame for a minute. How would you have responded? The person you saw dead just ten days before . . .

The person you witnessed hanging limp on a cross, with pericardial fluid flowing from the hole a Roman soldier bored into his side by thrusting a spear up under his ribcage . . .

The man you saw lifelessly extracted from the lumber he'd been nailed to, taken down, wrapped in burial clothes, which included completely covering his oral and nasal passages . . .

The one you have loved deeply and followed faithfully for two-and-a-half years has just entered the room. And he didn't get there by walking through the door; he somehow tessered through the *wall.* That man has just strode up to you, exhaled on you, wished peace upon you, and showed you the still-moist and vacant holes in his hands. How would you respond?

Thomas' response has been passed down throughout history. *Thomas responded to him, "My Lord and my God!"*[16] It was his only plausible response.

15 John 20:26–27.
16 John 20:28.

What convinced Thomas to believe was the tangible, physical evidence in front of him: Jesus was standing there. He could hear his voice. He could see his wounds. There was even the offer to let him touch them if he needed to.

Arthur Conan Doyle, the creator of Sherlock Holmes said, "When you have eliminated all which is impossible, then whatever remains, however improbable, must be the truth."[17]

Thomas, the skeptical, but rational thinker, *had* to believe.

Jesus' final words to Thomas were, *"Because you have seen me, you have believed. Blessed are those who have not seen and yet believe."*[18]

CHANGED LIVES

Today, evidence for Christ's divinity comes in different forms. We can't see Jesus in the flesh or touch his wounds. But God created us with high-functioning brains. He knew we would need tangible proof in order to believe and trust in him. So, that's what he's given us. People who need proof that Jesus really is the Messiah can find it in six different areas of evidence. Each of these forms of proof are different from each other. Together, they form an encouraging case for believing that Jesus really is who he claims to be.

The first proof is really what this book is all about: *changed lives*. Thomas' life is just one of those, as Jesus had dozens upon dozens of

17 Doyle, Arthur Conan: *The Adventure of the Blanched Soldier*, a short story included in *The Case-Book of Sherlock Holmes*, UK 1926 edition, p. 1011.

18 John 20:29.

social encounters during his earthly ministry.[19] Beyond these, over the past 2,000 years, more than two billion lives have been changed by Jesus.[20]

These lives, personally touched, have, in turn, changed history.

He's Not the Only One

Three decades ago, I moved my family from rural Colorado to the seaside city of Oceanside, California, to plant a brand-new church. I did so because I had come to believe that Jesus really was, and is, the Savior of the world and holds the greatest hope for every person's life and eternity.

A few months after moving in, I met a young father, whom I'll call "Robert." Robert and his family were also new to the area, and open to new friendships. Robert's wife was spiritually open, but Robert himself had reservations. At his wife's prompting, the two of them joined a small Bible-study group I was putting together.

This couple met with me for about three months before the public launch of our church. Our meetings were simple. We'd read a portion of Scripture about the life of Jesus, and then we'd talk about what we saw there.

When the church began holding public services, my young couple

19 For an enumeration of these, see my list of **101 Personal Encounters with Jesus** in the End Notes.

20 Seed, Hal: *The God Questions,* Outreach Inc., 2009, p. 117 & 123. The website www.adherents.com (currently inactive) counted present day Christians on the earth as 2,000,000,000. This estimate does not include all of those who lived between AD 33 and 2009.

friends attended, but spiritually, Robert held back. In his words, "I definitely wasn't ready to become a Christian."

Later that year, an evangelist held a big campaign at Jack Murphy Stadium, the then-home of the San Diego Chargers. Robert attended. He told me afterwards, "It was really something,"

"How so?" I asked.

"Well, when the speaker gave an invitation to receive Christ, thousands of people went forward. I couldn't believe it!"

"Why not?"

"I just couldn't imagine making a decision like that so quickly. I need time to process," he said.

With the church up and running, I suddenly had lots on my plate. I lost track of Robert for a while. I saw him in the congregation most Sundays, but we didn't get a chance to connect for a bit. Then one Sunday we bumped into each other after the service. Robert said something that made me think he was starting to see the world through the eyes of a Christ-follower.

"Robert," I said, "what you just said sounds like you've started to believe."

"I have," he said.

"When did that happen?" I asked.

"I'm not sure," he said. "But sometime over the last few months I've become a Christian. I can't tell you exactly when or how it happened, but I'm definitely a believer."

My friend never had the chance to see the nail holes in Jesus' hands, nor to put his fingers in the Lord's side, but through reading and thinking and watching others who'd come to faith, Robert accumulated enough evidence to place his faith in Christ.

In my experience, most people who come to believe have a significant moment when they encounter the Lord, like Thomas, and pronounce him "My Lord and my God!" But God reveals himself uniquely to each person who seeks him. Robert's experience was more of a slow-and-steady movement, until he realized that somewhere in his journey he'd crossed a line and come to believe without consciously realizing it.

Fast-forward thirty years, and my friend is still walking faithfully with the Lord. His son and daughter are grown, and both have strong relationships with the Lord. In fact, Robert's daughter works on a church staff these days!

SOCIAL PROOF

Churches, like the one Robert's daughter works at, do tremendous good in their communities. You might think of churches as simply groups of people that meet for worship, but they do so much more. Most provide counseling for people in need. And food for those who are hungry. Many create ministries to aid in addiction recovery. Robert's daughter coordinates her church's help for the homeless in their area.

For the first 300 years after Christ's resurrection, Christianity was illegal throughout the Roman Empire. But once it became legalized, churches could start to own buildings. So church leaders from all over the Empire got together and decreed that everywhere they built a cathedral (a really big church, in a metropolitan area), they would also build a hospital next door. This is why even today so many hospitals bear Christian names, like "St. Jude's," or "St. Paul's," or "Mount Sinai."

After Thomas' encounter with the risen Christ, he traveled widely to share his faith. Hundreds of thousands of believers have done so since then. Where they go, they bring not only the good news of Jesus, but modern medicine to cure tropical diseases, and water purification systems to prevent diseases. It was Christians who invented the concept of charitable organizations. Think of the Red Cross, the Salvation Army, the Young Men's Christian Association (YMCA), Compassion International, Samaritan's Purse, World Vision, Bread for the World. It's estimated that 95 percent of all charities have been started by Christians.[21]

It was Christianity that invented education for the masses. It's likely you've heard of Charlemagne and "The Carolingian Renaissance." Charlemagne was an eighth-century ruler who united most of Western Europe for a time. In AD 800, Pope Leo III gave him the title "Holy Roman Emperor." Charlemagne established free public education for all the children in his realm. He did so because he wanted them to be able to learn about the God of the Bible. Psalm 139:14 says humans are "remarkably and wondrously made" with great mental capacity. Charlemagne wanted his subjects to be able to develop that capacity.

21 This figure is cited both by D. James Kennedy in *What If Jesus Had Never Been Born?* Thomas Nelson, 2008; and John Ortberg in *Who Is This Man?* Zondervan, 2012.

This belief in nurturing the mind is so important that in America, 93 percent of all private colleges were founded by Christians.[22]

THE EVIDENCE OF THOMAS' LIFE

Thomas' belief was enough to propel him to martyrdom. Thomas was so convinced that Jesus Christ was the Messiah come from God to save the world from our sins that he spent the rest of his life traveling to tell others this incredible news. Though he had never previously left the confines of his very small country, the Twin traveled to Syria, then Iraq, then Sri Lanka, and finally to South India, where authorities there gave him a choice: *recant your belief, or die.*[23]

Not recanting, he died of multiple spear wounds. Indian Christians call the place of his martyrdom, "The Mount Saint Thomas." It's a small hillock in Tamil Nadu, India. You can visit it today. In a bit of a twist of fate, the grave of the man who needed tangible evidence serves as a small piece of evidence for us that Jesus really did live, and really is the Messiah.

22 Ibid.

23 https://en.wikipedia.org/wiki/Thomas_the_Apostle.

CHAPTER 2

An Outsider Looking In

THE STORY OF PHOTINI

We don't think about it much, but indoor plumbing is one of the wonders of the modern world. People in developed nations have little understanding of the constant drudgery of life without a sink and faucet. Cooking, cleaning, washing dishes, and even brushing your teeth are all exercises in conservation when every ounce of H_2O must be trundled home on one's head.

A gallon weighs over eight pounds. Pour five of those into a ceramic pot and you've got one massive burden to schlep home on your head. In most pre-plumbing households, the responsibility for conveying liquid to the home falls on the woman of the house, or one or two of her daughters, if she has them.

Misery loves company, so water-bearers often meet up early in the morning to make the task less tedious. That's how it went in ancient times in the Samaritan village of Sychar. There was a lot of foot traffic at 6 a.m., making its way to Jacob's Well. This famous well is a half-mile south of town. I visited it several years ago.

The gospel of John, Chapter 4, holds the story of an infamous woman who visited this famous well on a day Jesus happened by.

For some reason, Western Christians identify her generically as "The Woman at the Well." Eastern Christians have given her the name *Photini.*[24]

Photini either had no daughters, or they were all grown and gone. It was her job to haul water home every day. This little lady had a pretty hard life, as we'll see in a minute.

One reason women fetch water early in the day is to get the chore over with. Mark Twain once said, "If you have to eat a live frog, do it first thing in the morning. Then nothing worse will happen to you for the rest of the day."[25] Water-fetchers have followed this advice since long before it was given.

Israel is situated in a semi-arid climate zone along the coast of the Mediterranean. Afternoons can get unpleasantly hot. A second reason to get the chore over with in the morning is to avoid the heat of the day.

Every morning, as the women gathered for water duty, Photini avoided the camaraderie and stayed home. She went to the well at noon because she preferred being alone. People can be cruel. She'd learned to avoid human interaction as much as possible.

SHAME

Along with carrying water, Photini carried a heavy load of shame. Shame can be debilitating. If you've experienced it, you know that

24 https://en.wikipedia.org/wiki/Samaritan_woman_at_the_well.

25 Tracy, B. (2007). *Eat That Frog!* San Francisco, CA: Berrett-Koehler Publishers, Second Edition, p.2.

it's painful. Packed up with shame are feelings of powerlessness, worthlessness, distrust, and discouragement.

Shame was ever-present with Photini. Like all Middle Eastern girls of that day, she dreamed of her wedding day. But for whatever reason (either death or rejection), her first marriage didn't work out. Nor did the second. Nor the third. Nor the fourth. By the time she met Jesus, the woman at the well had had five marriages, and was living with a man out of wedlock.

Middle Easterners live in what is called an "honor-shame culture." Maintaining one's honor, and one's family honor, is paramount. Bringing shame on yourself is terrible. You'll be looked down on, talked about, and shunned. Bringing shame on your village is worse. And because Middle Eastern villagers have a sense that what one does reflects well or badly on the entire village, Photini lived with the village's condemnation every day.

That's why she skipped the morning water run and went by herself at noon. Despite the heat. Despite the loneliness. And maybe it's a good thing she did. Because on this particular day, she had a conversation with a man who changed everything for her, and for her village.

PHOTINI—THE WOMAN AT THE WELL

He [Jesus] left Judea and went again to Galilee. He had to travel through Samaria; so he came to a town of Samaria called Sychar near the property that Jacob had given his son Joseph. Jacob's well was there, and Jesus, worn out from his journey, sat down at the well. It was about noon.

A woman of Samaria came to draw water.

"Give me a drink," Jesus said to her, 8 *because his disciples had gone into town to buy food.*

"How is it that you, a Jew, ask for a drink from me, a Samaritan woman?" she asked him. For Jews do not associate with Samaritans.

Jesus answered, "If you knew the gift of God, and who is saying to you, 'Give me a drink,' you would ask him, and he would give you living water."

"Sir," said the woman, "you don't even have a bucket, and the well is deep. So where do you get this 'living water'? You aren't greater than our father Jacob, are you? He gave us the well and drank from it himself, as did his sons and livestock."

Jesus said, "Everyone who drinks from this water will get thirsty again. But whoever drinks from the water that I will give him will never get thirsty again. In fact, the water I will give him will become a well of water springing up in him for eternal life."

"Sir," the woman said to him, "give me this water so that I won't get thirsty and come here to draw water."

"Go call your husband," he told her, "and come back here."

"I don't have a husband," she answered.

"You have correctly said, 'I don't have a husband,'" Jesus said. "For

you've had five husbands, and the man you now have is not your husband. What you have said is true."

"Sir," the woman replied, "I see that you are a prophet. Our ancestors worshiped on this mountain, but you Jews say that the place to worship is in Jerusalem."

Jesus told her, "Believe me, woman, an hour is coming when you will worship the Father neither on this mountain nor in Jerusalem. You Samaritans worship what you do not know. We worship what we do know, because salvation is from the Jews. But an hour is coming, and is now here, when the true worshipers will worship the Father in Spirit and in truth. Yes, the Father wants such people to worship him. God is spirit, and those who worship him must worship in Spirit and in truth."

The woman said to him, "I know that the Messiah is coming" (who is called Christ).

"When he comes, he will explain everything to us."

Jesus told her, "I, the one speaking to you, am he."[26]

In six rounds of dialogue, Photini goes from a sad, self-conscious, shame-laden woman to a person of hope and light.

Round one: Much to her surprise, this unknown Jewish man initiates a conversation with her. "Who *are* you?" she thinks. "Jewish men don't speak to women they aren't related to, and they *never* speak to Samaritans."

Centuries earlier, the northern portion of Israel had been conquered by the Assyrians. Each time they defeated a country, they relocated some of its citizens to other conquered lands, replacing them with

26 John 4:3–26.

people from elsewhere. The idea was to mix up all the cultures in order to minimize uprisings and create one blended Assyrian culture. So the Jews of Samaria (formerly northern Israel) intermingled and intermarried with the imported peoples, altering their belief system. They were still monotheists, but their worship was different from classic Judaism. Hence, true Jews considered them in some ways worse than Gentiles. Samaritans were not to be trusted and not to be associated with. Knowing this Jewish disdain, the woman legitimately asks herself, "What kind of man is this who is asking me for a drink?"

Jesus has aroused her curiosity.

Round two: Jesus doesn't answer her question. Read other stories about Jesus and you'll see that he almost never answers a question. Instead of answering, he'll raise another question. That's what he does here.

If you knew the gift of God, and who is saying to you "Give me a drink," you would ask him, and he would give you living water.

Her whole life has been spent lugging water. "I want that!" she thinks. "Where do I get this living water?"

This idea takes her further in thinking about the stranger's identity. Her greatest ancestor was Jacob, whose name was eventually changed to Israel. "Are you greater than the founder of our nation?" she asks.

Jesus has deepened her curiosity.

Round three: Once again, Jesus doesn't answer her question. He expounds on the benefits of his offer of living water. *Everyone who drinks from this water will get thirsty again. But whoever drinks from the water that I will give him will never get thirsty again.*

Okay, more intrigue. She's now not only interested, she's also a customer. *Sir, give me this water so I won't have to come here to draw anymore.*

Round four: Jesus wants her to know that he knows her and cares about her situation. He deepens the conversation. *Go call your husband.*

Now, the shame: *I don't have a husband.*

Jesus has moved from someone to wonder about, to someone she's willing to trust with her darkest secret. "I have no husband. I'm alone. I'm an unwanted woman. I don't measure up." Women in that culture could not get a job. As an unmarried woman, she had no status. She's dependent on others for everything she has.

Round five: Jesus shocks her by telling her something he couldn't have possibly known.

You have correctly said, "I don't have a husband." For you've had five husbands, and the man you now have is not your husband.

Oh my! How could he have known this? Who *is* this man?

She wants to know more, but she's also afraid. She asks her burning question: *I see that you are a prophet.* (Implied: "Are you?") Then, she deflects by asking a theological question. *Our ancestors worshiped on this mountain, but you Jews say that the place of worship is in Jerusalem.* (Implied: "Who's right?")

Final round: Jesus deflects her deflection. "The most important question isn't *where* you should worship, but *how* you should worship." The elephant in the room remains. He's told her entire familial history, something no human could possibly do without help.

She addresses the elephant. *I know the Messiah is coming.* What she's politely asking is, "Are you him?"

Twenty-seven sentences. Fifteen by Jesus, twelve by the woman. In these twenty-seven sentences she's gone from self-conscious and shame-filled to curious and hopeful.

One more sentence seals her transformation. *I, the one speaking to you, am he.*

It's a sentence of confirmation. "Yes. I am who you're suspecting I am. I am the One you've waited for all your life. I am the Messiah."

CONVINCED

In the course of a conversation by a well at noon, a shell of a woman undergoes a spiritual and emotional transformation. The woman who walked to the well by herself went back into town to gather everyone together.

Just then his disciples arrived, and they were amazed that he was talking with a woman. Yet no one said, "What do you want?" or "Why are you talking with her?"

Then the woman left her water jar, went into town, and told the people, "Come, see a man who told me everything I ever did. Could this be the Messiah?" They left the town and made their way to him.[27]

After one conversation with Jesus, the woman is no longer self-focused, self-deprecating, or self-defeated. Her shame has been lifted. Now she's thinking about her village. She strides back into town and convinces them all to come investigate Jesus for themselves. This is why Easterners call her *Photini.* The word means "Enlightened One" or "Bringer of Light."

27 John 4:27–30.

Once Photini saw who Jesus was, everything changed in her, and for her. She enlightened her entire village, and many of them believed.

Once Photini saw who Jesus was, everything changed in her, and for her.

Now many Samaritans from that town believed in him because of what the woman said when she testified, "He told me everything I ever did." So when the Samaritans came to him, they asked him to stay with them, and he stayed there two days. Many more believed because of what he said. And they told the woman, "We no longer believe because of what you said, since we have heard for ourselves and know that this really is the Savior of the world."[28]

Photini's one encounter with Jesus convinced her he was the Messiah.

BIBLICAL PROOF

Last chapter we said that, like Thomas, we all need proof to believe. One form of proof is the evidence from changed lives. A second form of proof that has helped millions over the centuries is the Bible itself. People who read the Bible discover it really is a book like no other. It changes them.

What convinced Photini that Jesus was Messiah was that he knew everything about her. When people read the Bible for the first time, they discover that it seems to know everything about them as well. Open a Bible and start reading and you'll discover that its words

28 John 4:39–42.

accurately describe your secret feelings, hopes, fears, and search for a sense of purpose.[29]

Hebrews 4:12 says, *The word of God is living and effective and sharper than any double-edged sword, penetrating as far as the separation of soul and spirit, joints and marrow. It is able to judge the thoughts and intentions of the heart.*

When I read the Bible, it's like the Bible is reading me.

Another astounding feature of the Bible is that most people who start reading it never stop reading it. They come back to it regularly, rereading passages they've seen before, but seeing new things each time they open it.

The Bible makes claims about itself that no other book makes. It claims to be God's divine revelation. 2 Timothy 3:16 says, *All Scripture is inspired by God.* That word *inspired*, in the original language, literally means "exhaled." It's saying that the words of each of the sixty-six books of the Bible were breathed out from the mind of God into the minds of the men who wrote them, so that the concepts God wanted communicated were done so flawlessly.

The Bible claims to be perfect. Psalm 12:2 says, *The words of the Lord are pure words, like silver refined in an earthen furnace, purified seven times.* That word *pure* can also mean "flawless." Silver that has been purified seven times has virtually all the dross removed. It's as pure as humanly possible. The Bible goes one further. It's wisdom and instruction with 100 percent of impurities removed.

29 For instance, read Psalm 139, Psalm 22, Psalm 23, or Psalm 8.

The Bible also claims to make us better. Watch what happens to people who read the Bible over several consecutive weeks, and you see that they are improved by it. They become kinder, more loving, less selfish, more interested in others.

People who read the Bible often also become smarter. The author of Psalm 119 testifies that reading Scripture has increased his I.Q.

Your command makes me wiser than my enemies, for it is always with me. I have more insight than all my teachers because your decrees are my meditation. I understand more than the elders because I obey your precepts.[30]

The author goes on to say that the Bible has become like a compass for his life, guiding him to see the right road before him, and to make good decisions. *Your word is a lamp for my feet and a light on my path,*[31] he says, as if when he reads it he's holding a roadmap or GPS in his hands.

This divinely inspired book claims that Jesus is Messiah. While this may not be a convincing argument by itself, when you set this proof beside the proof of so many lives that seem to have been changed by Jesus, and the proofs we'll cover in the coming chapters, together they point to the probability that he just might be the One we've all been looking for.

STACY WASHINGTON-PAIGE'S STORY

Photini had an encounter at a well that changed her immediately. Stacy Washington-Paige had one in a park that took a little longer.

30 Psalm 119:98–100.
31 Psalm 119:105.

Stacy is a Marine wife, and a member of my church. I called her to ask her if I could include her story here, and she agreed. Ask we talked, she said to me, "Like the woman at the well, I had felt like an outsider my whole life. And I don't anymore."

Growing up in Maryland, Stacy met and married her husband, Lonnie, and moved with him to Quantico, Virginia, and then Philadelphia, and then Oceanside, California.

She told me, "A few weeks after we'd moved into our new home, I was feeling lonely. I couldn't find any friends, so one day I decided to take my daughters to the park. I was raising my daughters to be Wiccans, so we looked a little different and acted a little differently. The other moms at the park didn't want talk to me.

"And then I met Alyssa. She was sitting under the slide, having tacos with her children. Alyssa asked me questions. She was wearing a shirt that said, "I Love My Church" on it, which told me that she was a Christian. I had had uncomfortable encounters with Christians before, so I was wary. But she made it easy. We had a nice conversation.

"At the end, instead of asking for my phone number, which would have felt threatening to me, she said, 'Hey, do you want to exchange Facebooks? No pressure.' I could tell she wanted to be my friend.

"The first time we hung out, it was a little scary. What do you wear to a mom play date? And what will she think of my Wiccan children? We hung out at the Play Kingdom.[32] Our conversation somehow came around to Star Wars, which led up to talking about religion, because we talked about 'The Force.'

32 The Play Kingdom is a mega jungle gym at my church.

"The Play Kingdom is inside the church building. That helped me see that I could be comfortable inside a church.

"The next time I came to the church was on Halloween. The church was a safe place to trick-or-treat. And when Alyssa mentioned they were having hot dogs, I said, 'I'm there!' Halloween is a big day for Wiccans, believing that the spirits of the other world come closer on this day. So before we came over to the church, my girls and I set out an offering for the spirits on our front porch.

"When we got to the Halloween party, music was playing, and kids were having a blast in the bounce houses they'd set up. I met several people from the church, and they all seemed normal and friendly. I started becoming friends with people who went to the church, though I still had no intention of ever going to a church service.

"One day Alyssa asked me to come to a church service with her. I said, 'You know I'm not a church person.' But she explained that her husband Bryan was going to be giving the sermon that Sunday, and he wanted some friends there to support him. So I agreed to come."

Stacy paused for a minute.

"I remember everything Bryan preached that day. It helped me! I found out that I liked church! I was happy. Even though I didn't believe, church became a moral compass for me. Every time I went, I learned something about myself, and about God, and about living. So I started going weekly. I felt like I needed to be there, even though I didn't believe in God. I needed to hear the messages. I needed it.

"I love children. Even though I wasn't a Christian, they let me help with Sunday School. One of the lessons was 'I am fearfully and wonderfully made.'[33] It struck a chord with me. I couldn't figure out what 'fearfully made' meant, which made me keep thinking about it. But what I learned was that God loved me. I matter to God.

"It took about nine months of attending church for me to receive Christ. I remember that moment. I had an 'out-of-body experience.' Justin (the associate pastor) was leading communion. He explained that Jesus' body was broken for me. I had sat through two or three communion services before, but never eaten the elements. This time was different. I finally got it: Jesus had given his life for me. I was so sad that Jesus went through all of that for me. I started ugly crying. I closed my eyes and let him into my life. When I reopened them a few seconds later, the light seemed different. It was brighter. Everything was new. I could feel God's love for me.

"For so long I had been denying. And now I knew *this* is all real. I told Alyssa I had received Christ, which was embarrassing, because for so long I had said I would never do that."

Stacy stopped to reflect for a minute.

"I thought, *Why would Jesus do this for me? He doesn't even know me.* Then I realized that he does know me! Suddenly, I didn't have to have all the answers anymore because I trusted him. I knew that he had all the answers, but I didn't have to know them all because I understood his love, and that was enough. I still want to know more, and I'm learning more. But even if I can't get all the answers, his love is enough for me."

33 Psalm 139:14, NIV.

Over the next few months, Stacy's husband, Lonnie, admitted that he had received Christ as a child. "Lonnie got his faith renewed through my faith. He watched the changes in me, and that brought him back." Her children also have become Christians. And like Photini, Stacy is sharing her faith with others.

"I was with a lady the other day who grew up going to a church but had never experienced Jesus personally. I told her, 'You can. I talk with him all the time.' Now she calls me and tells me how wonderful it is to have a relationship with God."

THE FINAL CHAPTER OF PHOTINI'S STORY

The Eastern Church calls Photini "The Mother of Evangelists," because after leading her village to Christ, she led her five sisters and two brothers to Christ. Many of them began leading others to Christ as well. Eventually, Photini left her village of Sychar to bring the light of Messiah to people elsewhere. For a time, she shared her story throughout Israel, then she sailed to Carthage to present the gospel there. Eventually, she made her way to Rome, where she shared her faith enough that Nero had her tortured and put to death for her faith.[34]

One conversation by a well, and one in a park, and everything changed. That's why Photini and Stacy call him *Messiah*.

34 https://knowyourmothers.com/photini-mother-of-evangelists.

CHAPTER 3

A Father Who Needed a Miracle

THE STORY OF JAIRUS

The story of Jairus is part of an *intercalation*—an insertion of one story inside another story to tell them both together.

Jairus was the leader of the synagogue in the seaside village of Capernaum. So, think of a man of some stature. The town was home to about 1,500. A man in his position knew just about everyone. You can be sure he was aware of the day Jesus became a resident.

The Messiah spent his childhood in Nazareth, which is twenty miles southwest of Capernaum. For reasons unknown to us, after Jesus' baptism in the Jordan and temptation in the wilderness, when he returned to the region of Galilee, instead of moving home, he relocated to Jairus' village.

Here's what his first day there looked like:

He went down to Capernaum, a town in Galilee, and was teaching them on the Sabbath. They were astonished at his teaching because his message had authority. In the synagogue there was a man with an unclean demonic spirit who cried out with a loud voice, "Leave us alone! What do you have to do with us, Jesus of Nazareth? Have you come to destroy us? I know who you are—the Holy One of God!"

But Jesus rebuked him and said, "Be silent and come out of him!" And throwing him down before them, the demon came out of him without hurting him at all.

Amazement came over them all, and they were saying to one another, "What is this message? For he commands the unclean spirits with authority and power, and they come out!" And news about him began to go out to every place in the vicinity.

After he left the synagogue, he entered Simon's house. Simon's mother-in-law was suffering from a high fever, and they asked him about her. So he stood over her and rebuked the fever, and it left her. She got up immediately and began to serve them.

When the sun was setting, all those who had anyone sick with various diseases brought them to him. As he laid his hands on each one of them, he healed them. Also, demons were coming out of many, shouting and saying, "You are the Son of God!" But he rebuked them and would not allow them to speak, because they knew he was the Messiah.[35]

Jairus watched all this happen. Did these events convince him that Jesus was the Messiah? Probably not. But soon thereafter, his daughter got sick. Very sick. She was dying, and there was nothing Jairus, or Mrs. Jairus could do about it, except pray.

Somewhere amid his nightmare, it occurred to this village leader that there was one more thing he could do: he could appeal to the young Rabbi who had miraculously healed so many of his townspeople. The only problem was, Jesus wasn't *in* town at that moment.

35 Luke 4:31–41.

During that period of Jesus' ministry, he used Capernaum as a kind of a base of operations. Most days found him in other villages, teaching and caring for people. Jairus had great need of this miracle worker, but the miracle worker wasn't home.

Rumor had it that Jesus was on the east side of the lake, in what was called "The Decapolis," Gentile territory. Just before returning home, the gospel of Luke tells us he restored the sanity of a notoriously troubled man by casting a legend of demons out of him.[36]

Sailing home with his disciples, Jesus was met by an energized crowd. Jairus was among them, waiting anxiously. In desperation, he pleaded with the Rabbi to come and cure his daughter. "By all means," said Jesus. Together they made their way through the crowd.

JESUS IN CAPERNAUM

This is where the intercalation comes in.

When Jesus returned, the crowd welcomed him, for they were all expecting him. Just then, a man named Jairus came. He was a leader of the synagogue. He fell down at Jesus' feet and pleaded with him to come to his house, because he had an only daughter about twelve years old, and she was dying.

While he was going, the crowds were nearly crushing him. A woman suffering from bleeding for twelve years, who had spent all she had on doctors and yet could not be healed by any, approached from behind and touched the end of his robe. Instantly her bleeding stopped.

"Who touched me?" Jesus asked.

36 Luke 8:26–39.

When they all denied it, Peter said, "Master, the crowds are hemming you in and pressing against you."

"Someone did touch me," said Jesus. "I know that power has gone out from me." When the woman saw that she was discovered, she came trembling and fell down before him. In the presence of all the people, she declared the reason she had touched him and how she was instantly healed. "Daughter," he said to her, "your faith has saved you. Go in peace."

While he was still speaking, someone came from the synagogue leader's house and said, "Your daughter is dead. Don't bother the teacher anymore."

When Jesus heard it, he answered him, "Don't be afraid. Only believe, and she will be saved." After he came to the house, he let no one enter with him except Peter, John, James, and the child's father and mother. Everyone was crying and mourning for her. But he said, "Stop crying, because she is not dead but asleep."

They laughed at him, because they knew she was dead. So he took her by the hand and called out, "Child, get up!" Her spirit returned, and she got up at once. Then he gave orders that she be given something to eat. Her parents were astounded, but he instructed them to tell no one what had happened.[37]

The story within the story is the healing of the woman with twelve years of bleeding. Like Jairus, she waited at the shore, hoping against hope for a miracle.

The final book of the Old Testament, the book of Malachi, prophesies that when Messiah comes, he will "rise with healing in his

37 Luke 8:40–56.

wings."[38] When you're near a computer sometime, search for a picture of a "Jewish prayer shawl." You'll see that it's shaped like an elongated blanket, with a tassel dangling from each corner. When you wrap the shawl around yourself, these tassels hang down near your ankles. Jews call these tassels, "wings."

This troubled lady knew Malachi's prophecy. She believed that if she could just touch "the end of his robe" (i.e., one of his *wings*), she would be healed. Working her way through the crowd, she got within inches of Jesus. Bending down quickly, she wrapped her hand around one of his tassels just a second. That's all it took. She was healed!

Jesus was never content simply healing a person's body. He was interested in their hearts and minds and souls, so naturally, he wanted to talk with whomever had been healed and help their faith grow further. He also didn't want whoever it was to walk away feeling guilty for "stealing a healing." Meanwhile, the clock was ticking for Jairus and his daughter!

Daughter, your faith has saved you. Go in peace.

Jairus' heart must have palpitated as Jesus seemingly wasted precious minutes discovering this woman's identity and pronouncing her whole. It must have dropped out of his chest when his friend appeared and reported, *Your daughter is dead.*

I'm impressed Jairus stayed quiet while Jesus talked with the woman. His heart must have been in his throat as he watched precious moments pass while his little girl's life was in danger. It was Peter who

38 Malachi 4:2.

spoke up. (Peter was always speaking up. Talking out of turn may have been one of his spiritual gifts.) Jairus said nothing. He knew that Jesus knew what was at stake.

I'm even more impressed that Jairus said nothing when his friend announced the news of his daughter's passing. Imagine the anguish. His worst nightmare had just come true. He must have wanted to scream and yell and cry and pound his fists on something all at the same time. But apparently, he didn't. This deeply religious man loved his daughter and had devout faith in God. In silence, he began the internal process of meshing his faith with his loss when Jesus spoke.

Don't be afraid. Only believe, and she will be saved.

At this point, Jairus' brain went on tilt. "My daughter is dead. I'll never hold her again. . . Wait! What is he saying?"

The few minutes' walk back to his house seemed like an eternity. Then there was wading through the crowd of well-meaning mourners, the clearing of the room, and finally, the unfathomable words, *Child, get up!*

The text says, *Her spirit returned, and she got up at once.* I don't know what it looked like as "her spirit returned," but it was memorable enough that the three disciples who were present bore witness that it really happened.

Jesus, once again concerned not just for a person's body, but for her whole being, requested food be brought in. It's likely she hadn't eaten during the final stages of her illness, and he wanted to rectify this before everyone got caught up in the miracle. But whether while fetching the food or after delivering it, they very much got caught up in the miracle! *Her parents were astounded . . .*

In his conversation with Jairus, Jesus prophesies an event that was fulfilled within the hour.

And that's why they called him *Messiah.*

PROPHETIC PROOF

On another palpable note, along with the validation of millions of changed lives and the inner witness of the Bible, a third area of proof that points to Jesus' Messiahship is *prophecy*. Fourteen hundred years before Jesus was born, Moses predicted that the Coming One would be a prophet.[39] In the middle of their well-side conversation, Photini realized that Jesus was a prophet.[40] In his conversation with Jairus, Jesus prophesies an event that was fulfilled within the hour. *She will be saved,* he predicted. And minutes later, she was!

39 Deuteronomy 18:18.
40 John 4:19.

The phenomenon of fulfilled biblical prophecy has convinced many that its assertion of Jesus' Messiahship is true. Scholars have identified 1,817 prophecies on a widespread number of topics within the pages of Scripture.[41] If even one of these does not come true, then the Bible can't fulfill its claim of infallibility, and its contention that Jesus is Messiah falls suspect. So far, it's upheld its claims.

Here's an example. The book of Daniel, Chapter 11, describes 135 geopolitical events in and around the Middle East that will take place. All 135 were fulfilled between two hundred and four hundred years after Daniel recorded them.[42] The possibility of getting all 135 of these predictions right is so remote that anti-supernaturalists propose the book of Daniel must have been written by someone centuries after Daniel's death. Yet the accuracy of Daniel's descriptions of events and culture of his time (sixth century B.C.) verify that he wrote the book that bears his name.

Here's another. The Old Testament contains hundreds of prophesies related to the coming Messiah; 332 of these were fulfilled in Christ's first coming.[43] Some years back, a curious math professor named Peter Stoner decided to calculate the odds that any one person could fulfill just eight prophesies predicted of the Messiah. After diligent calculations, Stoner concluded, ". . . the chance that any man might

41 Payne, J. Barton; *Encyclopedia of Biblical Prophecy*, New York, Harper & Row, 1973.

42 Seed, Hal: *Future History,* Torrance, CA, New Song Press, 2007, pp. 144–145.

43 To see some of these for yourself, check out the listing of **Prophesies of the Coming Messiah** in the End Notes.

have lived down to the present time and fulfilled eight prophecies is 1 in 10^{17}" (1 in 100,000,000,000,000,000).[44]

That's a number so large it's hard to fathom. To help us understand its magnitude, Stoner devised an analogy. "Supposing we take 10^{17} silver dollars and lay them on the face of Texas. They will cover all of the state, two-feet deep. Now mark one of these silver dollars and stir the whole mass thoroughly, all over the state. Blindfold a man and tell him that he can travel as far as he wishes, but he must pick up one silver dollar and say that this is the right one. What chance would he have of getting the right one? 1 in 10^{17}."

Stoner went on to determine the likelihood that someone could fulfill forty-eight prophecies of Scripture. That number came to 1 in 10^{157}, a number so large it would fill too many lines for me to type out for you. For perspective, there are only 10^{80} atoms in our entire universe. And Jesus fulfilled not forty-eight, but 332 prophesies!

Far too many prophesies have been fulfilled to be considered coincidences. For objective thinkers, this is one more compelling reason to conclude, Jesus *must* be the Messiah!

JACK HAYFORD'S STORY

Back to the healing of Jairus' daughter. If God in the flesh could heal her, can and does he still heal people, albeit from heaven, in modern times?

In 1935, a young couple named Jack and Anita Hayford worried that their dearly loved baby (also named Jack) would die.

44 Stoner, Peter: *Science Speaks* (Chicago: Moody, 1963), quoted in McDowell, *Evidence That Demands a Verdict*, 175–176.

Younger Jack tells the story in his own words, "When I was one year old, I was supposed to die. When I was born, there was something wrong with my neck that the doctors couldn't fix, and it was inevitable that with the passage of time, the condition would have eventually twisted my neck and I would die. The doctor knew there was nothing he could do to change it.

"Five months, three times a week my mother took me for treatments to temporarily relieve my pain. But the doctor was so sure there wasn't anything that could be done to correct it, he only charged my folks for six treatments even though he administered somewhere between fifty and sixty.

"My parents didn't know the Lord. My mother's cousin didn't know the Lord either, but she'd heard about the Foursquare Church in Long Beach, California. She'd heard that at that church, Jesus healed people, and she wrote down what was wrong with me and took this note to the church. There she found somebody and asked, 'There's a little baby that's dying, and I brought this note. Will you pray for this baby?' The people said, 'We will.' They brought it into the Wednesday night prayer meeting of that church.

"The next day, my parents began to notice that things had changed. My mother's cousin had told her she'd taken a prayer request over to the church. Within the next few days, the doctor said, 'This baby is well. There is nothing wrong with him.' And not only did the doctor declare me well, but he also refused to take the money from my parents for the few payments he was going to charge, because, he said, 'I had nothing to do with the healing of this baby. This must have been something God did.'"[45]

Young Jack grew up and had a long and impactful ministry, serving as a pastor for decades. Though he recently passed, he left behind a legacy of faith, captured in the many books and hymns he wrote.

Jack wasn't raised from the dead, just miraculously saved from dying. His parents were not Christians at the time. This encounter moved them to pursue a relationship with Jesus and declare him to be their Savior. Miracles like this happen more often than you might think, which is another reason so many call him *Messiah.*

45 https://www.jackhayford.org/teaching/articles/my-personal-testimony-of-healing.

CHAPTER 4

A Sister Whose Brother Died

THE STORY OF MARY

Some years ago I ran across a fun fact about names during New Testament days. At that time, upwards of 50 percent of girls born in Israel were named "Mary." Jesus' mother, the mother of James the younger and Joses,[46] John Mark's mother,[47] the sister of Martha and Lazarus,[48] and Mary Magdalene,[49] all are prominent Marys within the accounts of Jesus' life. There's even a mention of a dynamic lady in Rome, who goes by the name of Mary.[50]

Each of the New Testament Marys had encounters with Jesus that convinced them he was the Messiah. In this chapter, I'd like to focus on just one Mary. She's sometimes called "Mary of Bethany," but more often, "Mary, the sister of Martha and Lazarus." This Mary is mentioned in three stories with Jesus. Each of them shines light on a particular attribute of Jesus that helps us understand not only why so

46 Mark 15:40.
47 Acts 12:12.
48 John 11:1.
49 Luke 8:2.
50 Romans 16:6.

many have concluded he's the Messiah, but why we've also concluded that he was a very likeable guy.

MARY—SISTER OF MARTHA AND LAZARUS

Mary's village of Bethany sits two miles east of Jerusalem. What happened there is so profound, we're still talking about it today. Though we don't know how, Mary and her siblings became such close friends with Jesus that he stayed with them whenever he visited the Holy City.

"The Right Choice"

Luke introduces us to her: *While they were traveling, he [Jesus] entered a village, and a woman named Martha welcomed him into her home. She had a sister named Mary, who also sat at the Lord's feet and was listening to what he said. But Martha was distracted by her many tasks, and she came up and asked, "Lord, don't you care that my sister has left me to serve alone? So tell her to give me a hand."*

The Lord answered her, "Martha, Martha, you are worried and upset about many things, but one thing is necessary. Mary has made the right choice, and it will not be taken away from her."[51]

Families are social microcosms unto themselves. Its members seem to intuitively figure out how to cover all the important personality types. So if the firstborn is an overachiever, the second born might become a jokester, and the third a beauty queen, or a ne'er-do-well. In this Bethany family, Martha occupied the position of "get things

51 Luke 10:38–42.

done," leaving Mary free to become the "hang out and learn" person. She was relationally inclined, while Martha was task oriented. As a task-oriented person myself, I feel a bit of a twinge of regret every time I read this story. I don't mind Jesus applauding Mary, I just wish he'd given Martha a little recognition for her hard work on everyone's behalf.

From first meeting, Mary was smitten by Jesus' teaching, and Jesus encouraged her to learn more. This was an age when women were seen as lesser-class citizens. The education of females was limited to the first few years of elementary school. They weren't allowed to hold jobs. In the second century A.D., Rabbi Judah bar Ilai added this to the Talmud's daily prayer list, "Blessed are you, Lord, our God, ruler of the universe who has not created me a woman."

Mary could see that Jesus believed women should be able to grow and learn. In the Lord's very first sermon in his hometown of Nazareth,[52] he read the prophesy of Isaiah 61, where Messiah proclaims that he has been anointed "to set free the oppressed." You might say Mary was "educationally repressed." Part of what Jesus was doing was setting this part of her free.

This took place in the fall of AD 32.

"That They May Believe"

The second mention of Mary comes three or four months later. This story involves Thomas, so we've seen a part of it already. The apostle John writes as an eyewitness:

52 Luke 4:16–18.

Now a man was sick—Lazarus from Bethany, the village of Mary and her sister Martha. Mary was the one who anointed the Lord with perfume and wiped his feet with her hair, and it was her brother Lazarus who was sick. So the sisters sent a message to him: "Lord, the one you love is sick."

When Jesus heard it, he said, "This sickness will not end in death but is for the glory of God, so that the Son of God may be glorified through it." Now Jesus loved Martha, her sister, and Lazarus. So when he heard that he was sick, he stayed two more days in the place where he was. Then after that, he said to the disciples, "Let's go to Judea again."

"Rabbi," the disciples told him, "just now the Jews tried to stone you, and you're going there again?"

"Aren't there twelve hours in a day?" Jesus answered. "If anyone walks during the day, he doesn't stumble, because he sees the light of this world. But if anyone walks during the night, he does stumble, because the light is not in him.

He said this, and then he told them, "Our friend Lazarus has fallen asleep, but I'm on my way to wake him up."

Then the disciples said to him, "Lord, if he has fallen asleep, he will get well."

Jesus, however, was speaking about his death, but they thought he was speaking about natural sleep. So Jesus then told them plainly, "Lazarus has died. I'm glad for you that I wasn't there so that you may believe. But let's go to him."

Then Thomas (called "Twin") said to his fellow disciples, "Let's go too so that we may die with him."[53]

53 John 11:1–16.

Lazarus was too sick for them to leave him, so Mary and Martha sent word to ask Jesus to come before it was too late. But Jesus didn't come. He had something greater in mind, so he intentionally lingered until Lazarus had passed away.

When Jesus arrived, he found that Lazarus had already been in the tomb four days. Bethany was near Jerusalem (less than two miles away). Many of the Jews had come to Martha and Mary to comfort them about their brother.

As soon as Martha heard that Jesus was coming, she went to meet him, but Mary remained seated in the house. Then Martha said to Jesus, "Lord, if you had been here, my brother wouldn't have died. Yet even now I know that whatever you ask from God, God will give you."

"Your brother will rise again," Jesus told her.

Martha said to him, "I know that he will rise again in the resurrection at the last day."

Jesus said to her, "I am the resurrection and the life. The one who believes in me, even if he dies, will live. Everyone who lives and believes in me will never die. Do you believe this?"

"Yes, Lord," she told him, "I believe you are the Messiah, the Son of God, who comes into the world."[54]

Even after his mild rebuke some weeks earlier, Martha held Jesus in great regard. She had faith in him, though her faith was about to be expanded!

Having said this, she went back and called her sister Mary, saying in private, "The Teacher is here and is calling for you."

54 John 11:17–27.

As soon as Mary heard this, she got up quickly and went to him. Jesus had not yet come into the village but was still in the place where Martha had met him. The Jews who were with her in the house consoling her saw that Mary got up quickly and went out. They followed her, supposing that she was going to the tomb to cry there.

As soon as Mary came to where Jesus was and saw him, she fell at his feet and told him, "Lord, if you had been here, my brother wouldn't have died!"

When Jesus saw her crying, and the Jews who had come with her crying, he was deeply moved in his spirit and troubled. "Where have you put him?" he asked.

"Lord," they told him, "come and see."

Jesus wept.

So the Jews said, "See how he loved him!" But some of them said, "Couldn't he who opened the blind man's eyes also have kept this man from dying?"[55]

Jesus wept is often noted as the shortest verse in the Bible. In their first encounter, Mary could see that Jesus cared about her learning. Now she, and everyone with her, can see that he cared wholeheartedly about people. At the risk of spoiling the next section when we read it, I'll tell you that Jesus is about to raise Lazarus from the dead. That's why he delayed in coming, and that's why he arrived now. He has this clearly in his mind while talking with Mary, yet he wept anyway. His sorrow at her sorrow moved him deeply. He couldn't stand how badly

55 John 11:28–37.

she and her friends were hurting, even though he knew he was going to relieve their hurt within a matter of minutes.

Then Jesus, deeply moved again, came to the tomb. It was a cave, and a stone was lying against it. "Remove the stone," Jesus said.

Martha, the dead man's sister, told him, "Lord, there is already a stench because he has been dead four days."

Jesus said to her, "Didn't I tell you that if you believed you would see the glory of God?"

So they removed the stone. Then Jesus raised his eyes and said, "Father, I thank you that you heard me. I know that you always hear me, but because of the crowd standing here I said this, so that they may believe you sent me." After he said this, he shouted with a loud voice, "Lazarus, come out!" The dead man came out bound hand and foot with linen strips and with his face wrapped in a cloth. Jesus said to them, "Unwrap him and let him go."[56]

After seeing this, I have to assume that everyone present came to believe that Jesus was the Messiah. Who else could re-energize a dead brain, re-start a lifeless heart, heal all the already-decayed flesh, and even neutralize the stench from a four-days-dead corpse?

It might be that several, if not all of them already believed even before Lazarus' resurrection. I say this because the stone that sealed his tomb weighed around two-thousand pounds. In my thirties, I tried to flip a rock one-tenth that size. It put me in the hospital. Moving

56 John 11:38–44.

Lazarus' burial stone took significant effort. If the people with Mary were hesitant about what they would find inside, I doubt they would have mustered the necessary willpower to roll it out of the way.

Whatever the case, they pushed that stone, and out popped Lazarus looking to all the world like a mummy. This helps explain Mary's third story, which takes place six days before Jesus' death.

A Special Anointing

Between stories two and three, Jesus headed back down to the Jordan Valley, where he did some of his final and most famous teaching. Then, just before Passover, he climbed the four-thousand-foot, twelve-mile assent again from Jericho to Jerusalem, and stopped off in Bethany the night before what we call "The Triumphal Entry," or "Palm Sunday."

Here's the story: Six days before the Passover, Jesus came to Bethany where Lazarus was, the one Jesus had raised from the dead. So they gave a dinner for him there; Martha was serving them, and Lazarus was one of those reclining at the table with him. Then Mary took a pound of perfume, pure and expensive nard, anointed Jesus's feet, and wiped his feet with her hair. So the house was filled with the fragrance of the perfume.

Then one of his disciples, Judas Iscariot (who was about to betray him), said, "Why wasn't this perfume sold for three hundred denarii and given to the poor?" He didn't say this because he cared about the poor but because he was a thief. He was in charge of the money-bag and would steal part of what was put in it.

Jesus answered, "Leave her alone; she has kept it for the day of my burial. For you always have the poor with you, but you do not always have me."[57]

> Mary's expression of love was beyond extravagant.

Mary's expression of love was beyond extravagant. The pure spikenard she poured over her feet came 3,000 miles, from India. It traded hands all along the way, and every time it traded hands, the new merchant put his markup on it. Google the phrase "value of denarii," and you'll get a wide variety of answers, mostly because few people take into account inflation over the years. If you search just right, you'll find that a denarius was "one day's wages for a skilled laborer." Say, a plumber, or a carpenter. These days, union plumbers and carpenters average $65,000 or $70,000 in annual salary, working approximately 250 days a year. At three hundred days' wages, Mary's perfume was worth about $80,000. Quite a gift for a woman living under Roman oppression!

I conclude from this that somewhere on Mary's mental and spiritual journey she decided that Jesus really was the Messiah. *Messiah* means "Anointed One." Knowing his death was imminent, she anointed his feet with the most expensive liquid she could find. Mary was convinced that Jesus was the *Messiah*.

And What of Lazarus?

Early church tradition has it that Lazarus lived another thirty years, and that he was so concerned about the condition of the unfortunate

57 John 12:1–8.

souls he spent time with during his four days in Hades that he never smiled again.

Walking around alive, Lazarus was living proof of Jesus' Messiahship, and therefore, a threat to those who opposed the new Christian movement. To avoid a second untimely death, Lazarus immigrated to the island of Cyprus. Twelve years later, when Barnabas and Saul arrived there,[58] they appointed him Bishop of Kition, a city on the southern coast of the island.

Upon his (second) death, Lazarus was buried there. In 649, Arab Muslims began their conquest of the island. For the next few centuries, Cyprus was jointly ruled by the Muslim Caliphate and Christian Byzantium. During the reign of Basil I, (867–886), Cyprus was freed from this dual-rule situation, and the Byzantines had time to do some restoring and reconstructing. A tomb was found bearing the inscription, "Lazarus, four days dead, friend of Christ."

The Byzantines loved collecting religious relics, so they exhumed Lazarus' remains and swept them off to Constantinople, where they could be visited by people on pilgrimages—at least until they were looted by French Crusaders in the thirteenth century, who in turn spirited them off to Marseille, where they were somehow lost.

To compensate the Cyprus Christians for their loss of Lazarus' sacred bones, Byzantine Emperor Leo VI had a magnificent domed church built over the site Lazarus had formerly occupied, naming it "The Church of Saint Lazarus." This Orthodox church became a

58 Acts 13:4.

Catholic church when the Venetians conquered the island, and then a mosque when the Ottoman Turks conquered it after them. In 1589, the Turks sold the building back to the Orthodox, so it's come full circle, albeit a bit worse for all the wear and tear of remodeling from one group to another. Such places are an archaeologist's dream.

HISTORICAL PROOF

Speaking of archeologists, the modern science of archaeology presents a fourth proof pointing to Jesus' Messiahship.

By the early 1800s, Great Britain had accumulated enough wealth that many of her richest citizens found themselves with time on their hands, which enabled them to begin pursuing discoveries in science and industry, and history. One such aristocrat was the Lady Hester Stanhope. In 1815, she sailed to the Holy Lands and began poking her shovel around the ancient Canaanite city of Ashkelon to see what might be discovered. Others followed.

Throughout the late nineteenth century, Brits and other western scholars were turning up dirt all over the Near East in hopes of finding artifacts and understanding the cultures of its previous inhabitants. By 1950 more than twenty-five thousand sites had been explored, revealing and confirming much about biblical history.

For instance, excavations at the cities of Mari, Nuzi, and Alalakh verified that Abraham's customs were consistent with his eighteenth-century BC culture. Digs in Hazor, Gezer, Megiddo, and Jerusalem confirmed the account of Joshua's conquest of Canaan, David and Solomon's building of the United Kingdom, the demise of Israelite power during the Divided Kingdom, and their subsequent exile to Babylon.

In archaeology's first one hundred fifty years, so much earth had been overturned that Dr. Nelson Glueck (who is not a Christian) pronounced, "Through the wealth of data uncovered by historical and archaeological research, we are able to measure the Bible's historical accuracy. In every case where its claim can be thus tested, the Bible proves to be accurate and reliable."[59]

A few years later, Dr. Jack Cottrell (a Christian) said, "It may be categorically stated that no archaeological discovery has ever controverted a biblical reference." In other words, what the Bible says about history is verified by what we've dug up, everywhere we've dug it up, and every time we've dug it up. Archaeology confirms the historic claims of Scripture.

Here's an example. According to the book of John, one of Jesus' great miracles was the healing of the cripple at the Pool of Bethesda.[60] Outside of the New Testament, no evidence had ever been found for such a pool. Skeptics ridiculed John's writing as fake news, "the obvious work of an imposter." Then, in 1888, traces of the pool were discovered near the church of Saint Anne. I've actually visited that pool. It's an active archaeological site to this day.

The gospel writer Luke was a medical doctor, so when he set out to record his account of the life of Christ, he *"carefully investigated everything from the very first, to write to you an orderly sequence . . . so that you may know the certainty of the things about which you were*

59 *Rivers in the Desert,* NY: Farrar, Strous and Cudahy, 1959, p. 31.
60 John 5:1–15.

instructed.'"[61] His careful investigation led him to benchmark his stories with specific names of rulers, officials, and events, which gave lots of details for critics to say "That never happened," and lots of opportunity for researchers to say, "Let's see what really happened."

For instance, Luke describes an Emperor-mandated enrollment of taxpayers throughout the entire Roman Empire.[62] He identifies Quirinius as governor of Syria.[63] He lists Lystra and Derbe as cities in the province of Lycaonia.[64] He names Lysanias as tetrarch of Abilene.[65] Each of these details was called into question by those who doubted the reliability of the Bible. Yet over time, each of Luke's statements has been verified by archaeological findings. Looking at all of this, Dr. Joseph Free has said, "Archaeology has confirmed countless passages that have been rejected by critics as unhistorical or contradictory to known facts."[66]

We may not be able to go back and touch Jesus' hands and side like Thomas, but we can touch stones and inscriptions and artifacts that help us believe that Jesus really is the Messiah.

ANOTHER SISTER

The ancient trio of Mary, Martha, and Lazarus reminds me of a more recent Dutch family who strengthened one another's faith through their own relationships with the Lord.

61 Luke 1:3–4.
62 Luke 2:1–2.
63 Luke 2:2.
64 Acts 14:6.
65 Luke 3:1.
66 *Archaeology and Bible History*, Wheaton: Scripture Press, 1969, p. 1.

In the early 1900s, Casper Ten Boom founded a watchmaking shop in Haarlem, Netherlands. The shop was on the ground floor, with living quarters for the family upstairs. I visited the shop some years ago.

Casper and his wife Cor raised four children. Cor died in her thirties. Two children married and moved away, leaving Casper and two daughters, Betsie and Corrie, to tend the shop and the home.

In 1940, Germany invaded Holland and began their systematic persecution of the Jews. Casper, Betsie, and Corrie believed that the Jews were God's chosen people, so when a Jewish lady knocked on their door and explained that her husband had been taken by the Nazis and her son had gone into hiding, the Ten Booms took her in. Soon they were providing shelter to a regular flow of Jews trying to escape persecution.

The Dutch underground built a secret hiding place inside Corrie's bedroom. It could hold up to six people at a time. A warning buzzer was installed in the house, giving time for refugees to make for the closet before Nazi inspectors could make it upstairs and find them.

On February 28, 1944, an informant notified the Nazis of the Ten Booms' activities. Casper, Betsie, and Corrie were arrested that afternoon. Casper died nine days later. Betsie and Corrie were taken to Ravensbruck Concentration Camp. Conditions were horrible there.

In Corrie's words, she "struggled with [her] faith." Why would God allow them to be treated this way? Of particular concern to her were the lice in the barracks. She vowed, "God tells us to give thanks in all things, but I will not thank him for the lice." A few days later she learned the reason the prison guards never entered their barracks: they wanted to avoid getting lice themselves. This privacy kept the women safe from abuse and also enabled the Ten Boom sisters to share their faith openly each evening. Corrie conceded, "I gave thanks for the lice."

Toward winter, Betsie's health was failing. She claimed she experienced three visions from God. The first was that they were to establish a home for former prisoners after their release. The second was to own a concentration camp where they could teach Germans to learn to love. The third was that they would be released before the New Year.

Betsie died fifteen days before the New Year, on December 16. Before passing, she told Corrie, "There is no pit so deep God is not deeper still." Five days before the New Year (on December 26), Corrie was given her release from the prison, on what was later discovered to be a clerical error.

After the war, Corrie set up a rehabilitation center for concentration camp survivors. In 1950, she transitioned the facility into a shelter for Dutchmen who were without work because they had collaborated with the Nazis. In ensuing years, Corrie spoke in more than sixty nations, telling the stories of God's miracles for her and her sister during their time in Ravensbruck. In 1975, World Wide Pictures released a film of her life called *The Hiding Place.* In 1967, Israel's Yad Vashem Remembrance Authority honored her as "Righteous Among the Nations." They added Casper and Betsie to that list in 2008.

HOW FAITH GROWS

Most people who encounter Jesus directly, or examine his claims through indirect means like science, prophecy, and archaeology, end up concluding that he really is the Messiah. Their spiritual journey begins there, but it doesn't end there.

After the woman with the bleeding problem was healed, Jesus strengthened her faith by talking with her for a few minutes. Spiritual journeys start with a direct encounter with Jesus (for Thomas and Photini), or an encounter with a follower of Jesus (like Stacy Washington-Paige), but that's only the start of the journey. Faith is like a muscle. The more it's exercised, the more it grows.

Sometimes God intervenes with growth exercises. He did that for Mary, at the resurrection of her brother. And he did that for Corrie. Both ladies already believed before God miraculously intervened. Jesus' work *after* we believe is one more reason *we call him Messiah.*

CHAPTER 5

A Scholar Who Had It Wrong

THE STORY OF SAUL

People who know a lot about a little tend to get passionate about their subject.

The history professor who has earned his doctorate in a specialized area of a certain culture, for instance. When questioned about one's area of expertise, it's easy to feel a little superior or get a little testy if someone disagrees with you. After all, what do they know? They haven't looked into it as deeply as you have.

Or the researcher who is the world's leading expert on the treatment of a particular type of cancer. To suggest a better treatment, well, think of the stakes! It could cost a patient their life, and you already know the best means for survival and recovery.

Or the programmer who excels in an efficient method of coding. Recommending a different way is met with resistance, and maybe some pushback.

The more you know about a matter, the more likely you are to be right, and the more likely you believe you're right, and the more likely you'll defend your knowledge. But, what if you're wrong? What if all your learning is off slightly?

That's the situation Saul of Tarsus found himself in on his way to Damascus. Born with what is likely one of the highest IQs of all time, coupled with some of the best education of his day, combined with a colossal sense of drive and purpose, Saul was on tilt at the idea that some of his fellow Jews were believing that the Messiah had come. According to everything he knew theologically, and he knew a lot, they were just plain wrong.

Tarsus was a leading city within the country that is now known as Turkey. Saul's parents were Jews who had managed to earn or buy Roman citizenship, something not easy to do in that day. They were either so wealthy or so valuable to the Empire that they bought or were granted citizenship with all the privileges it afforded. These were high-powered people.

Naturally, they wanted their gifted son to excel, attend the best schools, become a person of prominence someday. They sent him to boarding school in Jerusalem, the Holy City, to study under Gamaliel, the most renowned rabbi of the day.

Saul was about ten years younger than Jesus, meaning he graduated from rabbinical training soon after the Christian movement burst on the scene. Saul watched as every day, more and more of his kinsmen were converting. In doing so, in his mind, they were turning their backs on the God of Abraham, Isaac, and Jacob, forsaking their heritage as members of God's chosen nation, and forfeiting their place in the afterlife.

A DRAMATIC JESUS ENCOUNTER

Saul was concerned, frustrated, and mad. In his own words, *I was terribly enraged at them.*[67] He began to pursue these errant Israelites with a vengeance.

I myself was convinced that it was necessary to do many things in opposition to the name of Jesus of Nazareth. I actually did this in Jerusalem, and I locked up many of the saints in prison, since I had received authority from the chief priests. I was in agreement against them. In all the synagogues I often punished them and tried to make them blaspheme . . . I pursued them even to foreign cities.[68]

Of all the stories we're looking at together, Saul's is unique in that his first encounter with Jesus came after Christ's ascension to heaven.

"As I was traveling and approaching Damascus, about noon an intense light from heaven suddenly flashed around me. I fell to the ground and heard a voice saying to me, 'Saul, Saul, why are you persecuting me?'

"I answered, 'Who are you, Lord?'

"He said to me, 'I am Jesus of Nazareth, the one you are persecuting.' Now those who were with me saw the light, but they did not hear the voice of the one who was speaking to me.

"I said, 'What should I do, Lord?'

"The Lord told me, 'Get up and go into Damascus, and there you will be told everything that you have been assigned to do.'

"Since I couldn't see because of the brightness of the light, I was led by the hand by those who were with me, and went into Damascus. Someone

67 Acts 26:12.
68 Acts 26:9–11.

named Ananias, a devout man according to the law, who had a good reputation with all the Jews living there, came and stood by me and said, 'Brother Saul, regain your sight.' And in that very hour I looked up and saw him. And he said, 'The God of our ancestors has appointed you to know his will, to see the Righteous One, and to hear the words from his mouth, since you will be a witness for him to all people of what you have seen and heard. And now, why are you delaying? Get up and be baptized, and wash away your sins, calling on his name.'

"After I returned to Jerusalem and was praying in the temple, I fell into a trance and saw him telling me, 'Hurry and get out of Jerusalem quickly, because they will not accept your testimony about me.'

"But I said, 'Lord, they know that in synagogue after synagogue I had those who believed in you imprisoned and beaten. And when the blood of your witness Stephen was being shed, I stood there giving approval and guarding the clothes of those who killed him.'

"He said to me, 'Go, because I will send you far away to the Gentiles.'"[69]

This young scholar thought he was an expert in the subject of God. On his way to Damascus, he learned from the Source Himself that he was wrong.

The conversion of Saul of Tarsus to Paul the apostle is legendary. In one knockdown moment Saul was blinded, flattened, and flabbergasted by his supernatural meeting with Jesus. This young scholar thought he was an expert in the subject of God. On his way to

69 Acts 22:6–21.

Damascus, he learned from the Source Himself that he was wrong. The One the Jews were looking for really had come. Jesus really was the Messiah.

Saul's transformation was absolute and instantaneous. He went from persecutor to persuader in one brief exchange. This wasn't the only time Paul would hear from the Lord, but within a few days of this first encounter, he was not only a fully devoted follower of Jesus, but he was also preaching the Messiahship of Jesus in the synagogues of Damascus.[70] The man who had been imprisoning Jewish Christians began convincing nonbelieving Jews to become Christians.

The stubborn scholar became the unstoppable evangelist. Saul believed so firmly in Christ's Messiahship that he devoted the rest of his life to telling others about his Savior. After serving a stint as associate pastor in one of the first Gentile churches (Antioch), he began persuading people in Cyrus and Turkey. Then he crossed into Greece, where he met tremendous opposition. And not just the kind we see today, where people tell Christians to stop being pushy and forcing their religion on them.

Five times I received the forty lashes minus one from the Jews. Three times I was beaten with rods. Once I received a stoning. Three times I was shipwrecked. I have spent a night and a day in the open sea. On frequent journeys, I faced dangers from rivers, dangers from robbers, dangers from my own people, dangers from Gentiles, dangers in the city, dangers in the wilderness, dangers at sea, and dangers among false brothers; toil and

70 Acts 26:20.

hardship, many sleepless nights, hunger and thirst, often without food, cold, and without clothing.[71]

"Forty lashes minus one" is thirty-nine lashes. Five times thirty-nine equals 195. Imagine the texture of the skin on his back. Slick, lumpy, and inflexible. At some point it must have been difficult for Paul to get out of bed in the morning.

The word *Paul* means "little." He was likely less than five-foot-four.[72] How much room could there have been for whipping marks on his tiny back? Every inch must have been scar tissue. Every twist of his spine, every movement of his head was painful labor. Paul endured tremendous hardship for his conviction that Jesus really was the Messiah.

INTELLECTUAL PROOF

Like everyone with convictions, Paul needed significant proof to enable him to let go of his strongly held, but incorrect beliefs. Jesus supplied this with what is called an *epiphany*—an appearing, or manifestation of Christ. Epiphanies have happened throughout Christian history and are happening today in countries where Christian witnessing is barred or impeded. At this writing, Iran may be seeing more people come to Christ than any other nation on earth.

71 2 Corinthians 11:24–27.

72 Many websites tell us that the average first century Middle Eastern male stood 5' 5" [one example: https://www.quora.com/What-was-the-average-height-of-middle-eastern-men-during-Biblical-Times]. Saul's nickname, Paul, means "little," so he must have been under five-foot-five but by how much isn't actually known.

Most of these converts are coming to Christ in secret because it's illegal there to walk away from the Muslim faith. A large number of these secret conversions take place as a result of Jesus manifesting himself to individuals in their dreams.

In our culture, with open access to information, freedom to share our opinions, and an emphasis on logic, God seems to supply proofs for us in the ways we've already covered. He's provided social evidence through the witness of changed lives; internal evidence through experience when we read the Bible; supernatural evidence through inexplicably fulfilled prophecies; historical evidence through archaeology; and add one more to our list: intellectual evidence through the agreement of science with Scripture.

Science

There's a misconception these days that science is incompatible with Scripture and that scientists and faith don't mix. Let's clear both of these up.

First, the only times when science is incompatible with Scripture seems to be when scientific theory conflicts with Scripture. For instance, once upon a time, rational-thinking Europeans believed the world was flat. The Bible describes the Earth as a sphere—*"the circle of the earth"* (Isaiah 40:22). There was a lot of angst when Columbus cast off to sail across the Atlantic, until he sailed home.

Another seeming misalignment of science and Scripture started in AD 150, when the Egyptian astronomer Ptolemy catalogued 1,022 stars. For centuries people believed he had about the right number, in spite of the fact that Genesis 22:17 prophesied that Abraham's offspring would be . . . *as numerous as the stars of the sky and the sand on the seashore.* And Genesis 32:12 described the sand of the seashore as *too numerous to be counted.* Once telescopes were invented, scientists of course looked heavenward and confirmed the Bible's claims—the stars are too numerous to be counted. At last guess, the number is up to, well, *a lot.*

Dr. David Kornreich of Ithaca College describes it this way: "The simplest answer may be to estimate the number of stars in a typical galaxy, and then multiply that by the estimated number of galaxies in the universe, according to the European Space Agency (ESA). But even that is tricky, as some galaxies shine better in visible or some in infrared, for example. There also are estimation hurdles that must be overcome."[73]

To make at least a rough guess at it, Kornreich started with the round figure of ten trillion galaxies in the universe. He multiplied that by the Milky Way's approximately one hundred billion stars. What he came up with was *septillion* stars. It looks like this: 1,000,000,000,000, 000,000,000,000. The good professor then reiterated that this number was probably a ridiculous undercount, and that as our measuring devices become more advanced, so will the number of zeroes. I'd call that "*too numerous to be counted,*" wouldn't you?

To name a third science/Scripture conflict, for much of modern history, people thought the universe was in a steady, eternal, and

73 Harvey, Ailsa, and Howell, Elizabeth: *How Many Stars are in the Universe?,* https://www.space.com/26078-how-many-stars-are-there.html, 02/11/2022.

unchanging state. Yet Isaiah 40:22 claims that God *"stretches out the heavens."* In 1929, Edwin Hubble documented that the galaxies are moving away from each other in what we now know is an expanding, or *inflationary* universe. Our cosmic home is not only expanding, it's expanding at an exponential rate.

People who have not investigated the convergence of science and Scripture are often surprised that the Bible accurately describes,

- The conservation of mass and energy.[74]
- The hydraulic cycle of evaporation, condensation, and precipitation.[75]
- Gravity.[76]
- The Pleiades and Orion as gravitationally bound star groups.[77]
- The effect of emotions on physical health.[78]
  The spread of contagious disease by close contact.[79]
- The importance of sanitation to health.[80]

One more: For centuries, scientific theory was at odds with the first chapter of Genesis' description of the physical and biological development of Earth. Today, scientists are in substantial agreement

74 Ecclesiastes 1:9; 3:14–15.
75 Job 36:27–29.
76 Ecclesiastes 1:7; Isaiah 55:10.
77 Job 26:7; 38:31–33.
78 Proverbs 15:30; 16:24; 17:22.
79 Leviticus 13:45–46.
80 Numbers 19; Deuteronomy 23:12–13.

with the initial conditions of Genesis 1, as well as with subsequent events and the order in which they occurred.

After finding out about all this, planetary physicist and agnostic Robert Jastrow concluded, "For the scientist who has lived by his faith in the power of reason, the story ends like a bad dream. He has scaled the mountain of ignorance; he is about to conquer the highest peak; as he pulls himself over the final rock, he is greeted by a band of theologians who have been sitting there for centuries."[81]

Scientists

The second misconception is that scientists rarely believe in Jesus because science and faith don't mix. Polls suggest that about fifty percent of American scientists and three-quarters of doctors believe in a higher power.[82]

People who think this way rarely stop to consider that arguably the greatest scientist of all time (the G.O.A.T.), Sir Isaac Newton, was a committed Christian. He spent gobs of time studying Scripture and even put his hand to writing a few of his own commentaries.

Science and Christianity actually go so well together, that without Christianity, there might not be what we call "science," today. It was Francis Bacon, a committed Christian, who invented "the modern scientific method" of investigation.

81 Jastrow, Robert: *God and the Astronomers,* W.W. Norton & Company, 2000.

82 Worthen, Molly: *How Would You Prove That God Performed a Miracle,* New York Times, Dec. 2022.

If you remember from high school chemistry that a "faraday" is a unit of electric charge, you might be surprised to learn that its inventor, Michael Faraday, was a man of faith (as well as the developer of the science of electromagnetism). Building on his work, the theory of electromagnetism was completed by James Maxwell, also a Christian.

Consider these scientists within recent centuries: Johann Kepler, invented celestial mechanics; Roger Bacon (no relation to Francis), developed inductive reasoning; Albrecht von Halle, fathered modern physiology; Gregor Mendel, fathered modern genetics; all of them were Christians.

Two of the most important scientists of recent days are Georges Lemaitre, who coined the term "Big Bang," and Francis Collins, who shepherded the Human Genome Project. Both profess deep Christian faith.

And then there's the growing movement at a scientific think tank in California knows as *Reasons to Believe.* Hugh Ross is a Canadian astrophysicist who came to faith in the Messiah while studying cosmology at the University of British Columbia. As a child, he loved reading science textbooks of all kinds. He then studied the central holy books of Hinduism, Buddhism, and Zoroastrianism. His belief that a creation requires a Creator, and the consistencies of the Bible led him to conclude that Jesus was the Son of God. Ross completed a PhD in astronomy, then joined the faculty of Caltech, one of the most prestigious schools of science in the world.

Ross' ongoing studies of how the universe works led him to found an institute called *Reasons to Believe.* This working group of careful researchers has grown into a full-time faculty of faith-oriented scientists who devote their time to writing on every new scientific discovery, showing how each one substantiates the Bible's descriptions of the universe. Their mission is "to open people to the gospel by revealing God in science." At the time of this writing, their website (reasons.org) lists over fifty science scholars, 250 apologists, 140 other types of scholars, and more than 40 chapters of this organization worldwide.

When a scientific genius masters a diverse number of fields, he or she is labeled a "polymath." Aristotle, DaVinci, Einstein and Marie Curie were all polymaths, as was Blaise Pascal. Pascal made breakthroughs in several fields, including math, physics, and philosophy. His inventions include *Pascal's theorem* (on conics), *Pascal's Law* (of hydrostatics), *Pascal's calculator* (also known as *The Pascaline*), *Pascal's Triangle* (on mathematics), and *Pascal's barrel* (on hydrostatic pressure). Delving into probability theory, Pascal integrated his faith with science by coming up with *Pascal's Wager* which is about the existence of God. It goes like this: "Let us weigh the gain and the loss in wagering that God is. Let us estimate these two chances. If you gain, you gain all; if you lose, you lose nothing. Wager, then, without hesitation that He is."[83]

Ultimately, all ventures in both faith and science boil down to calculated probabilities. Wayne Gretzky, arguably the greatest hockey player of all time, weighed in on decisions of probability when he said, "You miss one hundred percent of the shots you don't take."

On the faith side, Jesus took all the risk out of a decision to follow him when he promised, *"Ask, and it will be given to you. Seek, and you*

83 Encyclopedia Britannica.

will find. Knock, and the door will be opened to you. For everyone who asks receives, and the one who seeks finds, and to the one who knocks, the door will be opened."[84]

And, "*You will know the truth, and the truth will set you free.*"[85]

If you're thinking about making the decision to make Jesus your Messiah, he is only one prayer away.

If you're thinking about making the decision to make Jesus your Messiah, he is only one prayer away. Invite him into your life by saying, "Lord Jesus, I believe you are the Messiah and Lord, and I want you to be mine. I invite you into my life to wash clean all my wrongs, and to lead me from now on."

The words of that prayer are not magical, but they are words God has waited all your life to hear from you, because he created you to have a close, personal, and permanent relationship with him. God is a gentleman. He will not force his way into your life; he waits to be invited. The prayer in the paragraph above is a means to do that. If (or when) you pray this or a similar invitational prayer, he promises to come into your life and to lead and guide you.

A RELUCTANT ENCOUNTER WITH JESUS

This is what happened for one of the brightest minds of the twentieth century. Like Paul, and many of the scientists we've mentioned, Clyde Staples (C.S.) Lewis was born into this world with intelligence, drive,

84 Matthew 7:7–8.
85 John 8:12.

and purpose. As he mastered his studies, he began to think (like most brilliant people do) that the way he saw the world was right. Losing his mother at an early age left him with a wounded heart, and like many people with deep childhood wounds, he found it easier to cast blame on God by choosing *not* to believe in him.

Lewis was a quiet professor at Oxford University. During World War II, the British Broadcasting Company asked him to do a series of radio lectures. People were so enamored with these broadcasts that Lewis became the second most famous person in all of England. Second only to Winston Churchill, who offered Lewis a special medal of recognition following World War II.[86]

Lewis's BBC lectures were later published in a book titled *Mere Christianity*. Some would say that it is the most powerful explanation of Christianity outside of the Bible itself.

Lewis was born in Northern Ireland. His mother died when he was seven years old. His father sent him to an English boarding school the next year. Lewis learned to read classic literature in five languages. At age nineteen, when he took the entrance exams for Oxford, his examiner stated that Lewis' exams were "the best ever seen" in the history of Oxford University,[87] and Oxford was founded in 1096.

Before he entered Oxford, he served in the British Army during World War I, where he was wounded three times in battle.

Lewis was an avowed atheist until the age of thirty. In 1916, in a letter written to a friend, he wrote, "I believe in no religion. There

86 Downing, David: *The Most Reluctant Convert*, Downers Grove, IL: InterVarsity Press, 2002, p. 12.

87 Ibid, p. 82.

is absolutely no proof for any of them, and from a philosophical standpoint Christianity is not even the best. All religions, that is, all mythologies to give them their proper name, are merely man's own invention."[88]

Like many professing atheists, Lewis did not believe there was a God, *but* he admitted that he resented God for not existing.[89]

While teaching at Oxford, Lewis decided to investigate the truth claims of Christianity. He did so because he developed friendships with Hugh Dyson and J.R.R. Tolkien, two men who were open about their belief in Jesus.

As Lewis got to know these two, he became persuaded that their faith was real. In summer of 1929, he became convinced that Jesus Christ really was an historic figure, and that he really did die on the cross as a substitute for the sins of the world. So Lewis bowed his head and invited Christ into his life.

Hebrews 11:13–14 speaks about a group of people who died before Jesus had come to Earth. *All these people were still living by faith when they died . . . And they admitted that they were aliens and strangers on earth. People who say such things show that they are looking for a country of their own.*

Lewis said, "I realized that all my life I was like that. I was looking for a country of my own."

Hebrews continues, *If they had been thinking of the country they had left, they would have had opportunity to return. Instead, they were longing*

88 Hooper, Walter, *C.S. Lewis: A Companion and Guide*, New York: HarperCollins, 1966, p. 9.

89 Downing, p. 51.

for a better country—a heavenly one. Therefore God is not ashamed to be called their God, for he has prepared a city for them.[90]

Lewis said that in Christ, he had found a "better country." His encounter with Jesus not only changed his life, but it also changed his eternity. It opened a better country for him: the country of heaven.

Lewis' admission about his inner struggle to change his beliefs echoes what must have happened similarly inside Paul's mind on the road to Damascus. Lewis said, "You must picture me alone in that room in Magdalen, night after night, feeling, whenever my mind lifted even for a second from my work, the steady, unrelenting approach of Him whom I so earnestly desired not to meet. That which I greatly feared had at last come upon me. In the Trinity Term of 1929 I gave in, and admitted that God was God, and knelt and prayed: perhaps, that night, the most dejected and reluctant convert in all England."[91]

Some would call Lewis the greatest author of the twentieth century. He published over forty books while he was alive. Twenty more were published after his death. Most of them are about faith in Jesus.

TRANSFORMED

Strong and smart people sometimes feel like they have a lot to lose if they admit they've been wrong, especially in the realm of spirituality. Saul of Tarsus had much to lose: his position within the religious community in Jerusalem, his reputation as the intellectual heir to the great Rabbi Gamaliel, his standing with his father and mother.

90 Hebrews 11:15–16.

91 Lewis: *Surprised by Joy*, pp. 228–229.

But his encounter with Jesus was so real, he knew he would have been intellectually dishonest to deny it. So, Paul accepted Jesus Christ as his Lord.

The New Testament is a collection of twenty-seven books, thirteen of them written by Paul. Many were written from prison cells. Nothing could dissuade Paul from his belief in Christ. And it all stemmed from one dramatic encounter of the road to Damascus. Likewise, after that night in Magdalen College, nothing could dissuade C.S. Lewis.

Far from losing, Saul, soon-to-be Paul, gained an even greater reputation. Worldwide, he is acclaimed as one of the greatest thinkers and most selfless and influential persons in history.

Once he gets hold of a person, Jesus changes so much about them for the better, and usually, that person begins to help others change for the better as well.

CHAPTER 6

A Soldier Who Believed

THE STORY OF A CENTURION

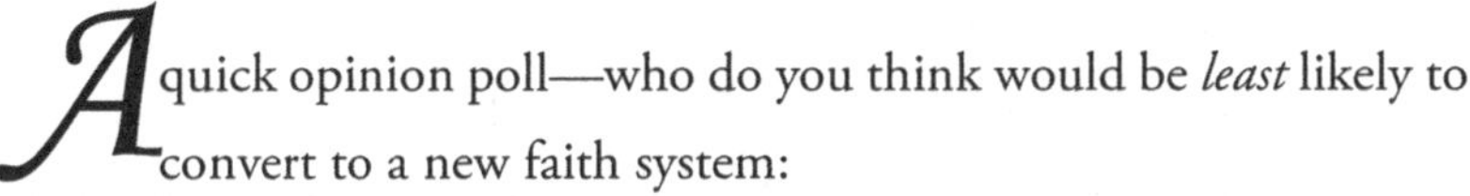

A quick opinion poll—who do you think would be *least* likely to convert to a new faith system:

- A man who was already part of that new faith system.
- A woman who felt like an outsider to her own faith group.
- A father whose daughter was healed by the leader of the new faith system.
- A sister whose brother was healed by the leader of the new faith system.
- A scholar who was a rising leader in the precursor to the new faith system.
- A soldier who was part of a very different faith system, and whose only exposure to this new movement was in watching its leader die.

I'll tell you what I think after I tell you about that last person on the list: the centurion.

ROME'S IRON FIST

The backbone of the Roman army was its *centuria* (plural for *centurion*). A Roman legion consisted of six thousand legionaries, divided into ten cohorts, each with six hundred men. Each cohort had six centuria commanding one hundred legionaries.

As vassals of the Romans, the Jews were not allowed to administer capital punishment. So when Jesus was sentenced to death, it was a Roman cohort that carried out the sentence, led by its centurion. This centurion played such a key role in the execution of the Messiah that he's mentioned in each of the first three gospels.

Matthew, Mark, and Luke all recount mostly the same details of the scene:

When it was noon, darkness came over the whole land until three in the afternoon. And at three Jesus cried out with a loud voice, "Eloi, Eloi, lemá sabachtháni?" which is translated, "My God, my God, why have you abandoned me?"

When some of those standing there heard this, they said, "See, he's calling for Elijah."

Someone ran and filled a sponge with sour wine, fixed it on a stick, offered him a drink, and said, "Let's see if Elijah comes to take him down."

Jesus let out a loud cry and breathed his last. Then the curtain of the temple was torn in two from top to bottom. When the centurion, who was standing opposite him, saw the way he breathed his last, he said, "Truly this man was the Son of God!"[92]

92 Mark 14:33–39.

This centurion was no slouch. He was a battle-hardened veteran who had killed enemies and seen comrades die. The centurion's job was to lead from the front. He was the first one up the hill, the first one over the wall, and the first one through the breach. On top of his helmet he wore a transverse crest (think big, feathered, half-moon, upside-down), so that his men could pick him out of a crowd and rally to him in the heat of battle. He was expected to display valor and be a source of inspiration for his legionaries. If he didn't, he could face execution.

Off the battlefield, his job was to train his legionaries, assign duties, mediate interpersonal conflicts and administer discipline. Centurions were sometimes appointed by the Senate, but more often, worked their way up through the ranks. Becoming a centurion usually took ten to twenty years. Depending on length of service, they were paid five to fifteen times a rank-and-file soldier.

Centurions had to be at least thirty years old, and literate (so they could read written orders). They had to be able to march twenty miles in five hours, in full armor, carrying a forty-five-pound kit.[93]

The other people we've profiled all saw Jesus at his best. This centurion saw Jesus at his worst. The first time he met Jesus was on the day of his crucifixion. He may have stood behind Pilate and witnessed the early morning trials. Pilate proclaimed Jesus innocent[94] and looked for ways to have him released.[95]

93 https://en.wikipedia.org/wiki/Centurion.
94 Luke 23:15.
95 Luke 23:23–25.

Our centurion saw Jesus stand with self-control as he was wrongly accused.[96] He was assigned to flog Jesus, a gruesome task that usually left men screaming, convulsing, and begging for mercy.

Then the governor's soldiers took Jesus into the governor's residence and gathered the whole company around him. They stripped him and dressed him in a scarlet robe. They twisted together a crown of thorns, put it on his head, and placed a staff in his right hand.

And they knelt down before him and mocked him: "Hail, king of the Jews!" Then they spat on him, took the staff, and kept hitting him on the head. After they had mocked him, they stripped him of the robe, put his own clothes on him, and led him away to crucify him.[97]

A man who could oversee such a brutal circus had to have ice in his veins. Try to read the following from the eyes of such a man:

As they led him away, they seized Simon, a Cyrenian, who was coming in from the country, and laid the cross on him to carry behind Jesus. A large crowd of people followed him, including women who were mourning and lamenting him. But turning to them, Jesus said, "Daughters of Jerusalem, do not weep for me, but weep for yourselves and your children. Look, the days are coming when they will say, 'Blessed are the women without children, the wombs that never bore, and the breasts that never nursed!' Then they will begin to say to the mountains, 'Fall on us!' and to the hills, 'Cover us!' For if they do these things when the wood is green, what will happen when it is dry?"

96 Matthew 27:13–14.
97 Matthew 27:27–31.

Two others—criminals—were also led away to be executed with him. When they arrived at the place called The Skull, they crucified him there, along with the criminals, one on the right and one on the left. Then Jesus said, "Father, forgive them, because they do not know what they are doing." And they divided his clothes and cast lots.

The people stood watching, and even the leaders were scoffing: "He saved others; let him save himself if this is God's Messiah, the Chosen One!" The soldiers also mocked him. They came offering him sour wine [37] and said, "If you are the king of the Jews, save yourself!"

An inscription was above him: This Is the King of the Jews.

Then one of the criminals hanging there began to yell insults at him: "Aren't you the Messiah? Save yourself and us!"

But the other answered, rebuking him: "Don't you even fear God, since you are undergoing the same punishment? We are punished justly, because we're getting back what we deserve for the things we did, but this man has done nothing wrong." Then he said, "Jesus, remember me when you come into your kingdom."

And he said to him, "Truly I tell you, today you will be with me in paradise."

It was now about noon, and darkness came over the whole land until three, because the sun's light failed. The curtain of the sanctuary was split down the middle. And Jesus called out with a loud voice, "Father, into your hands I entrust my spirit." Saying this, he breathed his last.[98]

98 Luke 23:26–46.

It's at this moment that Luke tells us, *When the centurion saw what happened, he began to glorify God . . .*[99] In Mark's version, it says, *he said, "Truly this man was the Son of God!"*[100]

A Change of Heart

Mr. Centurion was not predisposed to sympathize with Jesus. If he had been sympathetic toward his prisoner, he may have restrained his legionaries from their extracurricular humiliations of Jesus, like the scarlet robe they draped on his back, the crown of thorns, the staff in his hand, the feigned kneeling, the spittle, and the hitting on the head. When Pilate first gave the centurion charge of Jesus' execution, the Messiah was a mere object to him, not someone special, and certainly not the Son of God.

As Mr. Centurion led Jesus away, he was doing a job he had done dozens of times before, to dozens of other enemies of the state. Jesus was one of three criminals in his charge, nothing more, nothing less. As his men drove the stakes in Jesus' hands, as they lifted the cross and anchored it in the depression in the rock, even then, Christ was just another assignment to him. Why else would he have let his men cast lots for his clothes, scoff at his powerlessness, put a sign over his head that made fun of him and thrust the sponge to his mouth?[101]

But the death took six hours. So this centurion, who did not believe, had all that time to watch and form a different opinion.

99 Luke 23:47.

100 Mark 15:39.

101 Mark 14:36, a Roman soldier's standard gear included a sponge on a stick, which was used for cleaning oneself after going to the bathroom.

1. He noticed Jesus' nonresistance to his torture. Most men fought and cursed and begged and sobbed.
2. He noted Jesus' compassion toward the women. Most victims focused on their own misery on this journey. This man was thinking about others in the midst of his terrible pain.
3. He heard Jesus ask God to forgive his tormentors. At that moment, the centurion was his chief tormentor.
4. He watched the crowd scoff as Jesus fought for every breath. He noticed that this victim reacted to the jeers without malice or retaliatory remarks.
5. Then, he saw Jesus respond to the thief's request. He granted him entrance into heaven, as if it were his to endow.
6. Next, he watched nature itself mourn, as the sky darkened for the next three hours. That had never happened before.
7. And finally, he witnessed Jesus entrust his spirit to God, calling him "Father," like they were on a first-name basis.

One after another, these pictures made an impression on the centurion's mind. Deeply moved, but also soundly rational, he put them all together and concluded, "The one I have just executed is more than a man, he is God."

No further word is given about this centurion. But several of the details of Jesus' death take place out of sight of his followers. Who would have known what happened in Pilate's chambers during the trials there and reported it to the disciples? None of Jesus' followers were present in the soldiers' quarters during Christ's beating. How did they find out what happened there? Unless a Roman official told them about it, how could the record of these events have made their way into the writings of Matthew, Mark, and Luke? Our best bet is the centurion told them about all of it. Which means, he must have been so deeply moved by what he witnessed of Jesus' death, that he joined the newly forming movement called "the Way"[102] and later, "Christians."[103]

Back to our opinion poll. Thomas was determined to *not* believe without sensory evidence. But he wanted to believe. Photini was inclined to be suspicious of anyone outside her racial circle, but she at least believed that Messiah would come one day. Jairus and Mary both had prior contact with Jesus that led them to believe he was a rabbi with exceptional abilities.

Which leaves us with a religious zealot (Paul), and a pagan soldier (the centurion). Paul seemingly had everything to lose by changing his allegiance from Judaism to Jesus. People in modern cults are in a similar position. Few of them ever allow themselves to consider the claims of Christ objectively, but sometimes they do.

And the centurion? Roman religion taught that there was a pantheon of gods, all of them flawed and capricious. He had lived among the Jews long enough to know that they believed in only one

102 Acts 9:2.
103 Acts 11:26.

God. It's possible he had begun to consider their theological viewpoint before he met Jesus. But what a leap! From multiple gods to one God, who was in the flesh, at least until the centurion executed him.

I leave it to you. Is it a tie between Paul and the soldier? Or do you think one was a less likely convert than the other?

For me, both the scholar and the soldier seem like the longest of shots. The two of them coming from such different points of view and different persuasive circumstances, and both changing their minds so decisively is a fairly compelling proof that Jesus really was and is the Messiah.

SIX TYPES OF EVIDENCE

Why do people call Jesus *Messiah*?

In some ways, all humans are similar. But we differ in some important ways as well. One of the ways we differ is in how we process information and come to conclusions.

If there is a God who superintends the universe, then how we relate to him and get right with him is the most important bit of information we'll ever process and decide on. In Chapter 1 we saw that this was so important to Thomas that he refused to believe without proof he could touch. That option isn't available to us, but God knew that all of us would need tangible evidence just like Thomas did, and that some of us would need multiple types of evidence. So he supplied it for us.

One type of evidence is *social proof.* Over the past two thousand years, billions of people have had their lives changed by Jesus. That's a large number to grapple with. It's possible all these people were deluded.

Except, in Chapter 2 we learned that the creation of thousands of charities, hospitals, and educational institutions bear witness to people who were so changed by their relationship with Jesus that they devoted themselves to great causes in his name.

A second kind of evidence is *biblical proof.* In Chapter 3 we covered what happens when people read the Bible with an open heart. They find themselves hearing a voice inside of them alternately convicting and encouraging them about the kind of life they should be living. That internal voice is God's Holy Spirit.

A third variety of evidence is *prophetic proof.* In Chapter 4 we touched briefly on the hundreds of biblical prophecies fulfilled over the centuries. That number is too vast to be coincidence or orchestrated by human effort.

A fourth form of evidence is *historical proof.* Archaeology provides a kind of proof we can touch, as almost every time something gets dug up in the Middle East, it confirms some event or understanding about the Bible.

A fifth type of evidence is *intellectual proof.* As scientists investigate how our universe works, they generate lots of theorems and theories. The more science advances, the more it advances towards the Bible's description of how things work.

All of these encourage me that I'm on an intellectually tenable path—that Jesus really is the Messiah and worth trusting with my life and eternity.

But ultimately, the only evidence that matters to anyone is *personal proof.*

MY STORY

Personal proof happened for me on the evening of January 20, 1971. On the way home from a meeting where I had witnessed the interaction of real Christians for the first time, I invited Jesus into my life in the front seat of my swim team coach's VW Beetle.

I invited, and Jesus came in. I could feel his presence. My experience parallels Stacy's (in Chapter 2). The world literally looked different to me. Jesus said, *anyone who hears my word and believes him who sent me has eternal life and will not come under judgment but has passed from death to life.*[104]

I think that's why the light changed as I looked out the car window. I had passed from death (spiritual separation from God) to life (spiritual regeneration by God). The Bible says, *if anyone is in Christ, he is a new creation; the old has passed away, and see, the new has come!*[105]

Instantly, it seemed to me like the universe made sense: God made it and everything in it, and he made me and all people to have a person relationship with him. The world has a purpose, and my life has a purpose. I had never seen that before.

I went to bed late that night. As I woke in the morning, my first thought was, "Did that really happen to me?" I whispered quietly, "Lord, are you here? Did you really come into my life last night?"

As I did, I felt a chill down my spine and heard him whisper in my mind, "I am, and I did." I've asked those same questions a hundred times since, and I always get the same response. "Yes, I am, and I did."

104 John 5:24.
105 2 Corinthians 5:17.

Jesus isn't just an historic figure for me, or an intellectual construct, or a hope. He is with me every moment of every day. He is my *living proof.*

My wife, Lori, invited Jesus into her life at a Billy Graham Crusade in August of 1971. She would tell you that he is very much real because she experiences him personally every day.

My son, Bryan, invited Jesus into his life on April 19, 1992. He was four years old. I wasn't sure someone so young could even understand that Jesus had paid the price for his sins. But when Bryan asked if he could become a Christian, I took him into our bedroom and explained that Jesus took his spanking for him. I led him in a prayer, where he invited Jesus into his life, and much to my surprise, Lori and I noticed a change in him in the next few days. He wasn't a bad boy before, but he was a better boy after inviting Jesus into his life.

My daughter, Amy, prayed a similar prayer with Lori on December 16, 1992. She, too, was just four years old. I watched the same supernatural transformation happen to her that had happened to Bryan. Ask either of them if Jesus is real and they will say, "I know he is because I have experienced him personally."

We're but four of billions who have personal proof. The way to get personal proof is to ask for it, *personally.*

THIS IS *THE WAY*

John 1:12 in the Bible says *to all who did receive him, he gave them the right to be children of God, to those who believe in his name . . .*[106]

106 John 1:12.

This is why Christians say you must *receive* Christ. What they mean is, you must *receive* him into your life. You do that by inviting him in. He's a gentleman. He will not force his way in.

Capital punishment is a form of payment for the things a person has done wrong. Jesus, who never did anything wrong, took our capital punishment for us when he was executed on the cross. He paid for your wrongdoings, and mine, so we wouldn't have to pay for them ourselves. That's why all you must do is *receive.* You must receive what he already has done for you.

How do you do that? By praying a simple prayer. Something like, "Jesus, I receive what you did for me. You paid for my sin on the cross, and I receive it. And now, I want to become a child of God. I ask you to lead me from now on, as your child."

Jesus said, *Ask, and it will be given to you. Seek, and you will find. Knock, and the door will be opened to you.*[107]

If you just asked him into your life, he came in. So now, start talking to him, and listen. He'll start whispering to you, and you'll start experiencing him in other very personal ways. This is the personal proof you've needed. Now, live for him. Keep reading literature like this. And read the stories of Jesus for yourself, in the Bible. Find a church where they teach the Bible so you can learn from others who are further along the spiritual path than you are. Jesus never meant for us to live the Christian life alone.

107 Matthew 7:7.

As you grow in your new relationship with the Lord, you'll find yourself becoming more like Thomas, Photini, Jairus, Mary, Paul, and the Centurion, who all could say to others, "Jesus has changed my life, and I know he can change yours. And that's why I call him *Messiah.*"

"Jesus has changed my life, and I know he can change yours. And that's why I call him *Messiah.*"
- Hal Seed

END NOTES

1. 101 Personal Encounters with Jesus (as referenced in the Introduction and first chapter)

Listed by first appearance in Scripture:

1. Joseph–Matt. 1:25
2. Mary–Matt. 1:12
3. The Wise Men (the number, though popularly three, is unknown)–Matt. 2:1
4. John the Baptist–Matt. 2:14
5. Simon Peter–Matt. 4:18
6. Andrew–Matt. 4:18
7. James–Matt. 4:21
8. John–Matt. 4:21
9. A leper–Matt. 8:3
10. A centurion–Matt. 8:5
11. Peter's mother-in-law–Matt. 8:15
12. A scribe–Matt. 8:19
13. Another of his disciples–Matt. 8:21

14-15. Two Gadarene demoniacs–Matt. 8:29

16. A paralytic in Nazareth–Matt. 9:2
17. Matthew–Matt. 9:9
18. John's disciples–Matt. 9:14
19. A synagogue leader–Matt. 9:18

20. A woman with bleeding–Matt. 9:20
21. The dead daughter of the synagogue leader–Matt. 9:25
22-23. Two blind men–Matt. 9:28
24. A demon-possessed man–Matt. 9:32
25. Philip–Matt. 10:3
26. Bartholomew–Matt. 10:3
27. Thomas–Matt. 10:3
28. James son of Alphaeus–Matt. 10:3
29. Thaddeus–Matt. 10:3
30. Simon the Zealot–Matt. 10:4
31. Judas Iscariot–Matt. 10:4
32. A man with a shriveled hand–Matt. 12:10
33. A blind, mute, demon-possessed man–Matt. 12:22
34. Scribes and Pharisees–Matt. 12:38
35-38. His brothers (James, Jude, Joses, Simon)–Matt.12:46
39. Someone–Matt. 12:47
40. A Canaanite woman–Matt. 15:22
41. The Sadducees–Matt. 16:1
42. A child–Matt. 18:2
43. Children–Matt. 19:13
44. A rich young man–Matt. 19:16
45. Mary, mother of James and John–Matt. 20:20; 27:56
46. Two blind men–Matt. 20:29
47. The money changers–Matt. 21:12

48. The blind and the lame–Matt. 21:14

49-50. Chief priests (Caiaphas and Annas)– Matt. 21:23

51. Elders–Matt. 21:2

52. An expert in the law–Matt. 22:35

53. Simon the leper–Matt. 26:6

54. Woman with perfume–Matt. 26:7

55. High priest's servant–Matt. 26:51

56. Pilate–Matt. 27:11

57. Simon of Cyrene–Matt. 27:32

58-59. Two criminals on crosses–Matt. 27:38

60. Centurion executioner–Matt. 27:54

61. Mary Magdalene–Matt. 27:56; Mark 16:9; Luke 7:37

62. Joseph of Arimathea–Matt. 27:59

63. A man with an unclean spirit–Mark 1:23

64. Two disciples on road to Emmaus–Mark 16:13; Luke 24:13

65. The Shepherds–Luke 2:8

66. Simeon–Luke 2:25

67. Anna–Luke 2:26

68. People in the Temple, with the elders–Luke 2:47

69. Joanna–Luke 8:3

70. Susanna–Luke 8:3

71. Expert in the law–Luke 10:25

72. Martha–Luke 10:38

73. Mary–Luke 10:39

74. Woman from the crowd–Luke 11:27

75. Pharisee at dinner party–Luke 11:37
76. Someone in the crowd–Luke 11:13
77. Some people who reported news to Him–Luke 13:1
78. A woman with a disabling spirit–Luke 13:11
79. A synagogue leader–Luke 13:14
80. Someone on His way to Jerusalem–Luke 13:23
81. A leading Pharisee–Luke 14:1
82. One who reclined at table with Him–Luke 14:15
83. A Samaritan leper–Luke 17:16
84. People bringing infants to Him–Luke 18:15
85. Zacchaeus–Luke 19:2
86. The High Priest's servant–Luke 22:51
87. Men who were mocking Him–Luke 22:63
88. Herod–Luke 23:8
89. Centurion who executed Him–Luke 24:47
90. Servants at wedding in Cana–John 2:6
91. Headwaiter at wedding–John 2:10
92. Nicodemus–John 3:1
93. Woman at the well of Sychar–John 4:39
94. Royal official–John 4:50
95. Disabled man–John 5:9
96. Boy with loaves and fish–John 6:9
97. Adulteress woman–John 8:3
98. Man blind from birth–John 9:25
99. Lazarus–John 11:43
100. The crowd–John 12:17
101. Mary the wife of Clopas–John 19:25

2. Prophecies of the Coming Messiah (as referenced in Chapter 3)

PROPHECY	FULFILLMENT
Born of a woman, Gen. 3:15	Matt. 1:20; Gal. 4:4
Born of a virgin, Isa. 7:14	Matt. 1:18; Luke 1:26–35
Called, "The Son of God," Ps. 2:7	Matt. 3:17; 14:33; 16:16; 26:63
Seed of Abraham, Gen. 22:18	Matt. 1:1; Gal. 3:16
Son of Isaac, Gen. 21:12	Luke 3:23; Matt. 1:2
Son of Jacob, Num. 24:17	Luke 3:23; Matt. 1:2
Tribe of Judah, Gen. 49:10	Matt. 1:2; Heb. 7:14
Family line of Jesse, Isa. 11:1	Luke 3:23; Matt. 1:6
House of David, Jer. 23:5; Ps. 132:11	Luke 3:23; Matt. 9:27
Born at Bethlehem, Mic. 5:2	Matt. 2:1; Luke 2:4
Presented with gifts, Ps. 72:10	Matt. 2:1, 11
Herod kills children, Jer. 31:15	Matt. 2:16
His pre-existence, Mic. 5:2; Isa. 9:6	Col. 1:17; John 1:1; Rev. 1:17
He will be called Lord, Ps. 110:1	Luke 2:11; 20:41–44
He will be Immanuel, Isa. 7:14	Matt. 1:23; Luke 7:16
He will be a prophet, Deut. 18:18	Matt. 21:11; Luke 7:16; John 4:19
He will be a priest, Ps. 110:4	Heb. 3:1; 5:5–6
He will be a judge, Isa. 33:22	John 5:30; 2 Tim. 4:1
He will be a king, Ps. 2:6; Zech. 9:9	Matt. 27:37; 21:5; John 18:33–38

Anointed by Holy Spirit, Isa. 11:2	Matt. 3:16–17; Mark 1:10–11; John 1:32
His zeal for God, Ps. 69:9	John 2:15–17
Preceded by Messenger, Isa. 40:3	Matt. 3:1–2; 11:10; John 1:23
Ministry begins in Galilee, Isa. 9:1	Matt. 4:12, 13, 17
Ministry of miracles, Isa. 35:5–6	Matt. 9:32–33; Mark 7:33–35; John 5:5–9
Teacher of parables, Ps. 78:2	Matt. 13:34
Would enter the Temple, Mal. 3:1	Matt. 21:12
Enter Jerusalem on donkey, Zech. 9:9	Luke 19:35–37; Matt. 21:6–11
"Stone of Stumbling" to Jews, Ps. 118:22	1 Pet. 2:7; Rom. 9:32–33
"Light" to Gentiles, Isa. 60:3; 49:6	Acts 13:47–48
Resurrection, Ps. 16:10; 30:3; 41:10	Acts 2:31; Luke 24:46; Mark 16:6
Ascension, Ps. 68:18	Acts 1:9
Seated at right hand of God, Ps. 110:1	Heb. 1:3; Mark 16:19; Acts 2:34–35
Betrayed by a friend, Ps. 41:9; 55:12–14	Matt. 10:4; 26:49–50; John 13:21
Sold for thirty pieces of silver, Zech. 11:12	Matt. 26:15; 27:3
Money to be thrown in God's house, Zech. 11:13	Matt. 27:5

Price given for potter's field, Zech. 11:13	Matt. 27:7
Forsaken by His disciples, Zech. 13:7	Mark 14:50; 14:27
Accused by false witnesses, Ps. 35:11	Matt. 26:59–61
Dumb before accusers, Isa. 53:7	Matt. 27:12–19
Wounded and bruised, Isa. 53:5; Zech. 13:6	Matt. 27:26
Smitten and spit upon, Isa. 50:6; Mic. 5:1	Matt. 26:67; Luke 22:63
Mocked, Ps. 22:7–8	Matt. 27:31
Fell under the cross, Ps. 109:24–25	John 19:17; Luke 23:6; Matt. 27:31–32
Hands and feet pierced, Ps. 22:16; Zech. 12:10	Luke 23:33; John 20:25
Crucified with thieves, Isa. 53:12	Matt. 27:38; Mark 15:27–28
Prayed for His persecutors, Isa. 53:12	Luke 23:34
Rejected by His own people, Isa. 53:3	John 7:5, 48; Matt. 21:42–43
Friends stood afar off, Ps. 38:11	Luke 23:49; Mark 15:40; Matt. 27:55–56
People shook their heads, Ps. 109:25	Matt.27:39
Stared upon, Ps. 22:17	Luke 23:35

ABOUT THE CONTRIBUTORS

Writer

Hal Seed is the founding pastor of New Song Community Church in Oceanside, California. He and his wife, Lori, have two children, six grandchildren, and one large, obnoxious yellow cat.

Hal is the author of the best-selling *The God Questions* (500,000 copies in print), *The Bible Questions, Future History, Jonah,* and *I Love Sundays.* He helps pastors through his website www.pastormentor.com.

Project manager

Matthew Lockhart helps bring great books to life, having spent more than twenty-five years in leadership positions for noted Christian publishers including David C Cook, Standard, and Group.

Illustrations

A special thanks goes out to Scott and Mark for sharing select Bible art from their Providence Collection; artists featured in the works in this book include George Varian, Frank Soltesz, Arthur Becher, William Brassey Hole, and Harold Copping.